LOST & FOUND
CATHOLICS

Voices of Vatican II

Christopher M. Bellitto

ST. ANTHONY MESSENGER PRESS

Cincinnati, Ohio

Cover illustration and design by Aimee Sposito Martini,
Photonics Graphics
Electronic format and pagination by Sandy L. Digman
ISBN 0-86716-312-7

Published by St. Anthony Messenger Press
Printed in the U.S.A.

To my big brothers,

BOB AND ANTHONY—

They still show me the way.

Contents

ACKNOWLEDGMENTS

I am grateful to those who helped me tell our generation's story. Father Norman Perry, O.F.M., editor-in-chief of *St. Anthony Messenger*, ran a call for stories in his editor's column that produced many responses. Lisa Biedenbach, managing editor of St. Anthony Messenger Press, guided me with vision, calm professionalism and rejuvenating encouragement. Diane Houdek edited with clarity and skill. The Archbishop Corrigan Library staff at St. Joseph's Seminary, Dunwoodie, cheerfully responded to many requests even if they wondered why a medieval historian kept checking out modern statistics, psychology and sociology. I especially thank the voices of my fellow pilgrims themselves and those who gathered them. Their generosity and sincerity in sharing their stories is at the heart of this book. Many ended their letters with expressions of good luck and prayers for the project; some even thanked me for the chance to think through their own paths. One voice kept me going by writing, "May the blessing you receive today be the one you need most"—on a day when I really needed God's grace.

Most especially I thank my wife, Karen Bellitto, M.S.W., C.S.W., who read the voices and my several drafts with a sensitive, supportive and clinical eye. In our life as partners she helped me find my own voice and taught me how to sing in harmony.

Preface

One of the starting points for this book was the National Conference of Catholic Bishops' 1997 document *Sons and Daughters of the Light: A Pastoral Plan for Ministry with Young Adults*. The bishops' report contained snippets of comments from young adults who were surveyed as part of that study's background research. These young adults had in common an experience of Church that was historically distinctive, if not unique. Born in the decade before and the decade or two after the Second Vatican Council, we were formed—for good or ill—in a radically changing Church. The decades since Vatican II have been both tough and exciting, a time of great confusion and great possibility. Some of the opportunities paid off; others fizzled out. The older members of this first post-Vatican II generation have experienced two Churches; the younger ones have only known the Church as it has evolved after the Council.

Different members of our generation have dealt with these changing times in various ways. Some never left the Church. Others drifted away, but have come back or are thinking about it. Still more may want to return, but the Church they see is not the Church they remember from childhood. Some of us are so alienated from our baptisms that we explore cults, televangelists and New Age thinking. Our own faith has everything we are seeking, but, sadly, it appears we were never told. Many of us now want to know what we've been missing all these years. We are looking for our Catholic roots.

For the better part of a decade I've been interested in the subject of this book. I've spoken with and taught many young adults who wrestled with Catholicism, spent time away from the Church and have returned or are on their way back. I was just trying to understand how my personal experiences and struggles with the Catholic faith fit into the bigger picture of spiritual development and the Church at the end of the twentieth century. I found that I was not alone in my faith journey, and I wanted to share those insights.

Let me begin by outlining my own story here, especially since I say "we" and "us" frequently. Born in 1965, I went to Catholic schools through high school and deliberately chose a secular college. As I drifted between working as a journalist and high school teaching in my twenties, I wrestled with the idea of a priestly vocation. I spent a semester as a Jesuit novice where I learned that God wanted me to live a lay vocation. I took up graduate school, got married and am now a religion and history professor. Although my path did not include years of separation from the Church, I certainly did question basic aspects of my faith.

My field of academic research is Medieval Church history, but this book has allowed me to turn my historian's eyes and tools on my own generation. That's why I dare to pause in several places to give context to our experiences by summarizing the research of young adult ministers, spiritual directors, sociologists and psychologists. My hope was to relate in a popular (but not patronizing) style their insights for a general reader or a technical outsider like me.

This book is intended for two audiences. The first audience is made up of those who may be reaching back to the Church or trying to find a comfortable spot to call home. The second audience is composed of those who work with people returning to the Church, those who work with young adults and those who are responsible for parish adult education and outreach programs. Both audiences can find new insights and understanding from the stories and from the discussion of common patterns of spiritual and psychological development and the impact of Vatican II. Those who share this experience will be encouraged by hearing the voices of others who went through the same things; those whose experience of Vatican II took place at a different stage in their development can benefit from seeing the Council's changes through different eyes.

Before we settle in to listen to the voices of our generation, a word about this book's method is in order. We chose to focus on Catholics born between 1953 and 1973, although some valid points raised by slightly older people were taken into consideration, too, as were a couple of observations by the parents of our generation. A call for voices was placed in the "From the Editor" column of the January 1997 issue of *St. Anthony Messenger*, a magazine with a large national circulation. I sent letters and a similar call for voices to priests and laypeople who have been working to bring young adults back to the Church for many years and in various parts of the country—Chicago, Seattle, Boston, New Jersey and New York.

From these efforts, I received more than three dozen responses, stories of Catholics from twenty-one states and Canada. We used first names only, except where people asked not to be named at all, and kept identifying information to a minimum: a state or region, a profession, gender. We never intended an authoritative survey in terms of a mathematical or a representative sample. We wanted a snapshot, not a detailed landscape. We wanted to let the voices behind the statistics speak for themselves at greater length than they usually do in research studies. For statistical analysis, we rely on a few excellent recent studies of similar trends and age groups. The interested reader is encouraged to pursue these outside sources for more detailed and extensive research.

We measured the responses to our call for stories by three baselines. First, background reading and research often included bits and pieces of people's stories. Second, for several years while I thought about this book, I started conversations with many of my fellow young Catholics and even the parents of young Catholics at conferences, in the classroom and on other, more informal occasions. Third, I shared these voices with people who have extensive experience in young adult ministry for their feedback. They put some observations in context, offered caveats and noted what seemed common or out of the ordinary.

Finally, we decided to rely on some stories more than

others. This is because a few people chose to write longer accounts of their stories, often pausing to mention what they now see looking back or to reflect on what they've learned since then. While we went out of our way to avoid having a few people monopolize the conversation, we didn't want to limit those who repeatedly made important points. All the stories, whether or not the specifics found their way into the book, were taken seriously in the research and helped to back up general observations throughout.

I tried to showcase many sorts of voices from all areas of the spectrum: "right," "left" or "middle," whatever those labels mean. I ask that you do not look for a hidden agenda here or try to label this book, the research studies cited or the voices. Please do not hunt for codes, catch phrases or buzzwords. A variety of the perspectives that coexist in the Church today are here, either in my own words or someone else's. You'll agree with some, disagree with others, maybe even be angered or offended by a few. But the important thing is to hear all the voices if we are going to reconnect with the Church and with each other to lead the way into the third millennium.

A Portrait of the Post-Vatican II Catholic

> While I am truly sorry for the years I missed participating
> in Catholic theology and service, I feel my prodigal return
> is no less a miracle and a message. I hope my own road to
> return inspires other detached Catholics to consider
> reacquainting themselves with their Catholic roots. The
> rewards are eternal.

Don, forty-four, from Maryland says best why this book was written. He shares the story of how he went from feeling outcast and distanced from the Church to his return to participation in his parish. Don hopes that others who went through similar experiences will feel that they are not alone. He tells his story to invite others like him to take the first step toward reconnecting with their Catholicism and understanding the process of claiming a faith of one's own. Catholics of our generation have a distinctive experience of the Church, one that has significantly shaped the reasons we may have drifted away, as well as the reasons we may be returning. By looking at this experience, we may be better able to understand our own relationship with the Church or to serve those of our generation who are seeking an active role in the Church.

Our original call for stories asked for experiences of Catholics between the ages of twenty-five and forty-five leaving and returning to the Church, what some have termed the "lost generation." But it's important to remember that a good number of Catholics in our generation stuck with the Church as they—and the Church—tried to live out the challenges and changes of Vatican II. One voice from Michigan asked that the book keep in mind those who didn't leave the Church. There were other similar sentiments. From Tennessee, Michael reports that he's a thirty-five-year-old "cradle Catholic" who was never lost as were some in our generation. He knows a good deal about his faith, so he reaches to the Gospels to tell another side of our generation's story.

> I feel somewhat like the other son in the parable of the Prodigal Son. Just as I believe that there is much to be learned from those who left the Church and returned at some point, I believe that there is much to be learned from those of us who were raised in the same era yet stuck with the Church through it all. We recognized that, in spite of the imperfections that were described, the Roman Catholic Church provided an anchor for our faith lives. We brought our struggles to the Church and found support, rather than looking elsewhere before recognizing the value in Catholicism.
>
> I am not saying that we are better (or worse) than those who returned. I am just saying that we all bring different stories. I would hope that our messages can be as powerful as the stories of those who came back.

Michael's plea reminds us that we each have our own stories and perspectives. Although we belong to a group that was formed at a particular time in the history of the country and the Church, we are all individuals, as the many experiences and attitudes throughout the book will illustrate. Sometimes we best define our own experience when we hear someone else's story and think, "Yes, my experience was similar to that" or "No, that's not what I went through." As you read the stories, take some time to compare them to your own experience.

Crunching Some Numbers

Before we begin to hear the voices of our particular generation of Catholics, it's important to define what we're talking about. Who are we? What did we live through? What have been our formative social, political, cultural and—most important for this story—religious experiences? How did we react? What are our lives like now? It's only by knowing who we've been and who we are that we can then understand who we can become.

Once we get a general picture of our generation, we can explore in greater depth the lives of specific members of this generation. We'll also try to get a sense of where the experiences of individuals fit into the bigger picture of what it means to be a member of this generation of Catholics.

Without getting into too many mathematical nuances that don't concern us here, and without getting buried in statistics, we'll say that the generation we'll be hearing from in this book consists of those Catholics somewhere between the Baby-Boom generation and Generation X, overlapping with both. We were born between the early 1950's and the early 1970's. Most of us are in our thirties and forties, so we were born and grew up just before, during and after the Second Vatican Council.

A great deal of work has been done by sociologists and others on the Baby-Boom generation, Generation X and other segments of the American population. This collection of voices, while not a scientific study, relies on the data compiled and analyzed by such research teams. The general portrait that follows is culled from the impressions and conclusions on which many authoritative, careful researchers have already agreed.

Most experts say that Baby Boomers were born between 1946 and 1964, beginning when the GIs came back from World War II. These Baby Boomers, especially the older ones, were children and adolescents during the peace and prosperity of the Eisenhower years and became young adults in the tumultuous sixties. Wade Clark Roof has done a significant study entitled *A Generation of Seekers: The Spiritual Journeys of the Baby Boom Generation*. According to Roof, the Baby Boomers "value experience over beliefs, distrust institutions and leaders, stress personal fulfillment yet yearn for community, and are fluid in their allegiances—a new, truly distinct, and rather mysterious generation" (page 8).

While Baby Boomers are part of our generation, the first

wave of Generation X is the other. Generation X got its name from a novel by Douglas Coupland, *Generation X: Tales for an Accelerated Culture* (New York: St. Martin's Press), published in 1991. In it, three drifters in their twenties tell a series of disconnected, rambling, sullen stories to communicate their feelings of alienation, loneliness and lack of interest in family or job stability. The book is marked by a tone of oppressive apathy and negativism, but it was a popular success because it apparently struck a chord with many young people who identified with the rootless characters.

The *Young Adult Research Report*, prepared by Ron Bagley, C.J.M., and John Roberto, defined Generation X Catholics as those born between 1961 and 1981. Bagley and Roberto's report was partially based on research from a late 1995 survey of almost one thousand Generation X Catholics who were active in the Church; the survey was taken in Miami, San Diego, Philadelphia, Los Angeles, Omaha, Minneapolis, Dayton and Seattle.

Because the generation we're listening to in this book falls between the Boomers and the Xers, we'll be relying on these studies for background but adapting them as necessary to fit the generation that somehow fell between two more clearly defined groups. This, too, is part of the "lostness" of this generation.

The Times, They Were a-Changin'

In the 1960's, ground-shaking events took place on every level of society: politics (President Kennedy's assassination, President Johnson's Great Society program), racial and social events (the Civil Rights movements, the assassinations of Malcolm X and Martin Luther King, Jr., the 1968 riots outside the Democratic National Convention in Chicago, plus rioting in several major cities) and the war in Vietnam. The 1960's bled into the 1970's. Things didn't get better. Vietnam dragged on, which increased tensions between young people and their parents. Politics continued to sour, too, as Watergate shook our confidence. Economically, the gas lines grew longer in the early

1970's with the energy crisis. Then the 1980's went boom and bust.

It's a sad, complicated story. We became cynical, bitter, angry or let down. To use a word that keeps cropping up in both academic books and our own informal talks over coffee, we grew more and more *disillusioned* with—well, *everything*. Before we get labelled as a generation of whiners, however, let's consider whether our times are really any more or less cataclysmic than the three decades between the start of World War I and the end of World War II. Those years saw war on a truly international scale for the first time in 1914. The Roaring Twenties provided a brief respite, but the Great Depression soon hit. And shortly after the United States began to recover from the Depression, World War II erupted on an even bigger scale than World War I. The arms race began and ushered in the nuclear age.

While the events of our era aren't objectively more cataclysmic than other eras throughout history, what *does* seem to be true is that people *felt* different in the two eras. In the previous generations, everyone seemed to come together to fight a common enemy: the Depression, the Nazis, the Commies. In contrast, Baby Boomers, Generation Xers and those in between talk about floating alone through the events of the sixties, seventies and eighties. Deep splits in opinion on nearly every significant issue created a sense that the world was simply unraveling.

Roman Catholics, increasingly part of the wider society in which they lived, experienced the same upheavals. Andrea S. Williams and James D. Davidson of Purdue University surveyed Catholics in Indiana during the summer of 1993. Their work was the first stage of a large, nationwide study called the Catholic Pluralism Project. In their analysis, Williams and Davidson looked at the formative experiences of young adult Catholics.

> Catholics who grew up in the 1950's and 1960's experienced dramatic changes during their formative years. When they were coming of age, they knew both the tranquility of the post-war Eisenhower years and the

radical social movements of the 1960's. During the 1950's, they learned to have confidence in established institutions; in the 1960's, they learned to challenge them. In the 1950's, they learned to respect authority; in the 1960's, they questioned it. These "Baby Boomers" went from acceptance of established institutions to insistence on individuals' right to determine their own lifestyles, including their own religious beliefs and practices. ("Catholic Conceptions of Faith: A Generational Analysis," *Sociology of Religion* 57:3 [1996], pages 275-276.)

Vatican II

The times were changing in terms of religion, too. Our generation experienced a different Church from that of our parents because of the profound and sometimes confusing renewal ushered in by Vatican II. This Council was held in Rome from 1962 to 1965. Pope John XXIII (1958-1963) envisioned Vatican II as a new Pentecost. He was present at its first session in the fall of 1962. After his death the following spring, his successor, Pope Paul VI (1963-1978), oversaw the next three sessions of the Council and then was instrumental in putting its reforms into place. The changes brought about by the Council challenged the Church on every level.

The spirit of Vatican II was expressed by the Italian word *aggiornamento*, which is often translated into English as "updating" but literally means "to-day-ing," that is, bringing the Church in line with the world today, even as "today" changes every day. In fact, while Vatican II was a historical event of one place and time, Rome in the early 1960's, it is also an ongoing movement. John XXIII's new Pentecost is being lived out even now, over thirty years later.

As Williams and Davidson summed up the Council and its impact, Vatican II was "the most important event in the last one hundred years of Catholic history....a uniquely Catholic experience in the mid-1960's. No other American faith group experienced the anticipation, formulation and implementation of such dramatic changes. No other group experienced the radical change in religious worldview that the Council promulgated" ("Catholic Conceptions of Faith," page 277).

What happened as a result of Vatican II? Some Catholics growing up during that time say that it's easier to answer the question, "What *didn't* happen?" It felt like one thing was changing right after another within the Church, which had always been perceived as a rock even when society itself was shaking.

Most frequently people refer to the changes that took place at Mass: the prayers were said in English instead of Latin; the altar was turned around so the priest celebrated the Eucharist facing the people; in many cases the communion rails were removed; contemporary guitar music often replaced the more traditional organ and chant. The Church also relaxed or abolished rules such as no-meat Fridays and an insistence on head coverings for women in church. Familiar pious practices such as the rosary, novenas and Forty Hours devotion to the Blessed Sacrament were largely abandoned.

After Vatican II, the rigidity that had developed within the Church loosened a great deal. Laypeople became more involved in their parishes and dioceses. Catholics were urged to embrace the world and bring their faith to their workplaces, a change from the siege mentality that saw Catholicism as a safe haven in a dangerous, secular world. The Holy Spirit breathed over the whole world and Catholics were encouraged to share the Spirit with others, including Protestants and even non-Christians.

A good number of historians and observers of Catholicism agree that many of Vatican II's changes were extremely necessary, exciting and healthy. But as they look back now with the advantage of 20/20 hindsight, they say that many of the problems came about because the changes weren't always explained carefully when they were implemented. Many confused Catholics felt that what was true yesterday wasn't true today. How could that be? In some Catholic parishes and schools, the changes of Vatican II were only begrudgingly accepted while in other parishes and schools the pace of change accelerated almost daily. One Florida man in his thirties remembers with bitterness and anger the time his parish priest held up a rosary from the pulpit, declared, "We don't need these anymore!" and tore the string apart, scattering beads under the pews.

From the start, Vatican II was both a welcome period of updating and a confusing time. As we'll soon hear voices of our generation say, Vatican II has become a battleground. Some Catholics want the Council's changes to continue while others ask if the changes have gotten out of hand and are no longer in line with the spirit of the Council. For some, the legacy of Vatican II remains a wide-open opportunity; for others, it is still an open wound.

All Catholics were affected by it, but our generation was affected in a particular way, as we shall hear in the voices throughout this book. Not only did we have our own experience of the Council, but we were parented and taught by those who experienced the changes from a much different perspective.

Earning a Living While Living the Faith

Our generation of Catholics is different from our parents' generation in some important social, economic and religious ways. For instance, a 1993 study found that while twenty-one percent of Catholics who had been born between 1910 and 1940 attended college for at least a period of time, almost fifty percent of Catholics born between 1940 and 1980 had some college experience. That's one out of two younger Catholics with some college, as opposed to one out of five older Catholics.

In terms of what we do for a living, while less than ten percent of that older group of Catholics worked in white-collar jobs, about twenty percent of Catholics born between 1940 and 1980 are business owners or hold some type of professional position. In general, members of the younger generation of Catholics—Baby Boomers, Generation Xers or those somewhere in between—are better educated and make more money than members of the older generation of Catholics (William V. D'Antonio, et al., *Laity: American and Catholic. Transforming the Church*, page 71).

But while these statistics on education, profession and income seem to indicate progress and success, portraits of the religious activities of our generation of Catholics are more pessimistic. Almost sixty percent of the older generation of Catholics consider the Church to be important in their lives, but only about half of those born in the 1960's and 1970's say the same thing. Almost two-thirds of older Catholics attend Mass at least once each week, but only one in every four younger Catholics in this survey reported that they go to Mass every Sunday.

Beyond Mass attendance, there's a big difference between us and our parents or grandparents in terms of other religious activities. While ninety percent of our parents and grandparents in this survey pray every day, barely half of us turn our thoughts to talking with and listening to God on a daily basis. More than half of young Catholics think we can be good Catholics without marrying in the Church, going to Church every Sunday or giving money to help support a parish (*Laity: American and Catholic*, pages 76, 96).

In the midst of these statistics, however, there is reason for optimism, ironically, by returning to the subject of Mass attendance. Even though our generation goes to Mass less frequently, a 1993 survey conducted by the Gallup organization found that when adults between the ages of eighteen and twenty-nine do attend Mass, it's because we *want* to be there, not because we have to go. In that survey, almost seventy percent of young adult Catholics who had gone to Mass in the last week said that they went because they desired to go, compared to twenty-six percent who said they attended Mass because it was their obligation (reported in *Young Adult Research Report*, page 31). This indicates that when we go to church, it's because we have an adult sense that this is our chosen faith. Catholicism has become special and important to us personally. Although some readers may disdain the very notion that Catholics can stay away until they *want* to go to Church, at least it's a beginning.

The findings in the *Young Adult Research Report* are also extremely encouraging in terms of other areas of religious activities among our generation of Catholics. Once we've found our way back to the Church, it seems we're a very active group. Over eighty percent of young adult Catholics surveyed said that in a typical month they participate in a church-sponsored program or activity, attend worship services, and pray or meditate alone on a daily basis (*Young Adult Research Report*, pages 53-54).

Of course, statistics can be misleading. If the numbers in the *Young Adult Research Report* seem too optimistic, we can argue that those in *Laity: American and Catholic* appear too pessimistic. Perhaps it's wise to bear in mind Mark Twain's warning that there are three types of lies: lies, damn lies and statistics. Numbers don't always tell the whole story. Listening to the people represented by the statistics, hearing their stories, can clarify and give nuance to the general conclusions suggested by the statistics.

Searching for Ourselves

It seems that our generation of Catholics is still going through a volatile time. Although some of us have never left the Church, others drifted away—or perhaps even slammed the door behind us when we left. At the same time that some of us are coming back to the Church, others are still staying away and a few may be touching base and going off again in different directions. This kind of "spiritual surfing" is natural, as we'll see in Part One of this book.

For now, we'll quickly review what some experts in psychology see as the normal developmental tasks of young adults. Some of our drifting was simply part of growing up. While our individual stories may seem to describe a strange or confused path, taken together they reveal a common way of finding personal and religious meaning in life. God, it is often said, draws straight with crooked lines.

Once more, we'll rely on the *Young Adult Research Report*. In an article entitled "A Developmental View," Father Bagley discusses how young adults spend much personal time trying to figure out who they are, who they want to be, and how to achieve and then live the particular life they think is right for them. Bagley describes young adults as explorers. He also quotes an expert who calls young adults pioneers looking to settle into commitments that offer security and purpose because they want their lives to mean something.

Bagley studied a number of key psychologists and their theories to come up with his list of ten developmental tasks of young adults. We will summarize his ten tasks here because they describe well some of the essential characteristics, desires and struggles of young people in general and our generation of Catholics in particular. As developmental tasks, they remind us that we are pilgrims on a psychological and spiritual journey where getting there is part of the challenge.

1. *Becoming competent in interpersonal, social and professional skills* is perhaps the most basic task, since it is the foundation for the others.

2. *Achieving autonomy* means becoming a mature, independent, self-sufficient, self-directed, self-motivated and confident adult.

3. *Developing and implementing values* means working on values that are important to us because we choose, understand and embrace them for ourselves rather than having them imposed on us. We live according to certain values because they make sense, not because our parents told us to do so.

4. *Forming an identity* results in our having a strong sense of the kind of person we are and being comfortable with that person.

5. *Integrating sexuality into life* means understanding in an adult way who we are in terms of our sexuality and how our sexuality can be factored into healthy, positive relationships.

6. *Making friends and developing intimacy* is closely related to identity. But this task goes beyond our own identity. As we make friends and develop intimacy we're reaching out to

others who see the world as we do. Friends provide mutual support to one another.

7. *Choosing a marriage partner* often occurs both later and more deliberately for us than it did for our parents and grandparents.

8. *As we make initial job or career choices* in our twenties, we may try out different professions to find one that satisfies our desires and fits our personalities. This can be a time of searching for just the right occupation.

9. *Becoming an active community member and citizen* moves us beyond our personal lives and our families to meet broader responsibilities to our society. This can be a time of great idealism.

10. *Learning how to use leisure time* doesn't mean just learning how to relax or taking time to play. We decide what to do with our leisure time based on our commitments and what's important to us: to go back to school for further studies, to spend time with our families, to begin hobbies, to take care of our spiritual and/or physical well-being, or to help others.

Our generation's experiences emerge from this combination of tumultuous times, a changing Catholic population and the normal spiritual and psychological search for personal identity. We're faced with many—maybe too many—choices. We may have taken a time-out to drift a bit, but now we're looking for a safe place to land. The trouble is that we feel that the ground itself has shifted while we've been floating around.

On a religious and spiritual level, we may feel that we are shopping around a spiritual mall that offers us an almost endless supply of religious alternatives. Those of us who have little sense of our Catholicism and Catholic heritage may look to other traditions or trends because we're unaware of how our Catholic faith can lead us home.

Roof describes the situation of spiritual searching among Baby Boomers of many different faiths:

Religious and spiritual themes are surfacing in a rich variety of ways—in Eastern religions, in evangelical and fundamentalist teachings, in mysticism and New Age movements, in Goddess worship and other ancient religious rituals, in the mainline churches and synagogues, in Twelve-Step recovery groups, in concern about the environment, in holistic health and in personal and social transformation. Many within this generation who dropped out of churches and synagogues years ago are now shopping around for a congregation. They move freely in and out, across religious boundaries; many combine elements from various traditions to create their own personal, tailor-made meaning systems. Choice, so much a part of life for this generation, now expresses itself in dynamic and fluid religious styles (*A Generation of Seekers*, pages 4-5).

In this book, we'll hear from those who have drifted away in their search for meaning and from those who have done their searching without ever leaving home. And as we listen and learn, we will offer some direction for the ongoing search.

It's time now to let this generation of Catholics speak. As you listen to their voices, listen also for echoes of your own.

PART ONE

Drifting Away

How did our generation of Catholics experience Catholicism? Why have some stayed in the Church, while others have drifted away and still others are coming back with more enthusiasm than ever before? We will explore certain key aspects of our generation's experience to understand how we became disappointed, disillusioned and distanced from the Church, or felt that something was missing from our spiritual and religious lives. These experiences are many, including our religious education in school and a sense of being adrift in extremely troubled times. Our relationships with adults, teachers and each other changed as we all dealt with the impact of Vatican II.

Some of the drifting away that took place in our formative years was simply a result of growing up and questioning the traditions that had been handed down. People drifted in previous generations as well, although perhaps not to as great an extent when social and cultural expectations encouraged stability and tradition. For our generation, the turmoil of the 1960's, 1970's and 1980's led to far more doubt and questioning. Also, we are now beginning to realize that in many cases the tradition was simply not being handed down. We will hear this in many of the voices of our generation.

Blank Faces: Our Religious Education

One fundamental aspect of our generation's experience of growing up during the Vatican II era clearly stands out: our religious education—or lack of it. Many of our generation point out that we didn't receive a solid education in the faith.

Williams and Davidson report that when young adult Catholics in Indiana were brought together in groups as part of a research study, "their discussion of what they were taught actually turned into discussions of what they were not taught" ("Catholic Conceptions of Faith: A Generational Analysis," page 281.)

Jean Marie, thirty-five, recounted nine years of CCD classes in Vermont where she grew up:

> I wasn't challenged by the religious education materials provided. In fact, I didn't seem to understand what point was being made in the text nor how God related to it all. The feeling of loss slowly grew and my faith began to dwindle.

Part of the confusion seems to be that much of the emphasis after Vatican II was on an affective or emotional rather than intellectual dimension of faith. For example, while a fair number of us do remember lively retreats that helped us learn to pray, Susan from Missouri addressed the lack of teaching about prayer in her religious education:

> Overall I thought my Catholic education was, in a word, *pathetic*, and let me explain why. Sure, I learned how to recite the Our Father and the Hail Mary but no one—and I mean no one—ever explained to me how to pray, how to talk to God through petitioning and giving thanks for our blessings. Now, how am I supposed to develop a close relationship with God and Jesus if I don't know how to pray?...The main thrust of my Catholic education which included Catholic elementary school, high school, and college was that "God loves me." In my book, that is nice to know but [it] doesn't fill the hunger of knowledge that I have had for God all throughout my life.

The only way she finally began to learn how to pray "was that I accidentally read an article in our parish bulletin entitled, 'How we pray at St. Francis.' This happened when I was thirty-seven years old. I guess better late than never."

As children and adolescents in the post-Vatican II Church, we were often caught up in the music, life and sense of God's love. John XXIII spoke of Vatican II as opening the windows of the Church and letting in the fresh wind of the Spirit. How did we experience that in parishes and classrooms in the 1960's and 1970's? I recall standing up in my religion classroom in a New York City parochial school and singing "Kumbaya!" endlessly with a guitar-playing deacon, which seemed very cool at the time. In another song, we sang: "The *one* way to *peace* is the *power* of the *cross*" and flashed one finger, the peace sign, a fist and then made a cross with our index fingers.

At the time it was fun, but how educational were such exercises in terms of the substance of the faith? The games got us singing and dancing in the classroom and even in Church, which was the refreshing side of Vatican II. More than one member of our generation, on the other hand, looking back now at the religion classes of the late 1960's through the 1970's, used the cliché that the baby was thrown out with the bathwater when it came to the admittedly rote exercises of the *Baltimore Catechism*.

Some of us are beginning to hear and read about what we missed in terms of both the content and the expression of our faith. A 1993 survey in *Laity: American and Catholic* reveals that Catholics our age are not only uneducated about the Church, but we're increasingly aware of the lack of the most basic education in our faith, especially now that we are raising children of our own. When they ask, "Daddy, what's the deal with Mary being pregnant but she didn't have sex?", do we have a good answer, or any response at all?

Some fear that no lessons have been learned and that more Catholics will continue to drift away, creating yet another generation with no clear sense of what it means to be Catholic and of what Catholic teachings are. That's just what those young adult Catholics in Indiana were talking about. Moreover, we're often annoyed or embarrassed by our scanty knowledge of Catholicism, especially when we realize that members of other faiths are asking questions about Catholicism that we Catholics cannot answer ourselves. We might not even know what questions to ask.

A case in point: Jean Marie moved to eastern Virginia after

college, married and then settled with her husband in Louisiana, all the while drifting further away from the Catholic Church. After meeting Protestants in Virginia and then living as part of a distinct Catholic minority in Louisiana, Jean Marie realized that her childhood questions about Catholicism had never been answered.

> Once again, I began asking questions about Catholicism, especially asking those questions that Protestants were asking me and which I couldn't answer: Why do you believe the Pope has authority over you? How can the "wafer" be Jesus? Where does it say in Scripture that Mary is ever-virgin, that she was assumed into Heaven?

It was then, Jean Marie reports, that she realized she needed to find answers at last. She began reading a wide variety of sources, ranging from Richard McBrien (author of *Catholicism*) to Scott Hahn (author of *Rome Sweet Home*) to *The Catholic Controversy* of Saint Francis de Sales, and filled in her own blanks by attending RCIA (Rite of Christian Initiation for Adults) classes at her parish.

One woman in her early forties seems disappointed that she learned so little about Catholicism and prayer in her Catholic high school religion classes. She recalls:

> I think that they assumed that we'd already learned about the Catholic faith in grade school so our classes were things like comparative religion and life-through-films.... There wasn't any class that I can remember that helped me in any way to find a spiritual path for my life.

Other members of our generation have stronger feelings than the voices we've just heard. Some seem angry, feeling that they were cheated out of precious Catholic knowledge by parish schools, high schools or colleges. Teri is from southern California and is thirty-five years old. Writing about her drifting away from the Church with a passionate tone, Teri reports that she has finally found her faith by embracing aspects of what some might consider the "conservative" side of Catholicism, such as Latin Masses, traditional religious orders, and magazines, radio and TV programs with a traditional slant. Teri identifies herself as a traditionalist and in the past few years says that she's noticed "a growing network of young Catholics who are tired of liberal Church policies, and being subject to poor Catholic catechesis...."

> There is such a hunger for sound theology! And it is through study and networking, not, unfortunately, from the pulpits and lecterns that the youth are learning what it is to be authentically Catholic. My intention was not to offer a sermon concerning the status of young people [in] the Catholic Church. Yet given that I am one of the millions of youth who believe I've been cheated by a supposedly "Catholic" educational formation—twelve years of Catholic school and innumerable Catholic workshops—I have become a very vocal critic of the post-Vatican II Church as implemented in America....

While Teri's perspective is shared by some of our generation of Catholics, it may turn off other members of the same generation. Although the members of our generation share many common attitudes and experiences, we also cover a broad spectrum of beliefs. If we want to understand all sides of our experience as a group and find ways to come together in the Church, we need to listen respectfully to the varied voices. Teri further articulates the problems she sees in today's Church:

> Catholic youth must know the basics of their tradition. Without a solid education they won't know what they are leaving,.... I believe I was most blessed, that I had a strong Catholic foundation, so that even though I took a detour to a nondenominational church for a time, I did not end up on a one-way street with no sense or ability to even consider options. Most young Catholics don't have such an upbringing today.
>
> So many of the "education" programs that Catholicism offers today are not educational, other than to educate participants that what they have as Catholics is either outdated, outmoded or outright ridiculous. Psycho-babble, sharing your story, experiences and feelings have replaced the teaching of doctrine in many sermons and classrooms. Mass frequently becomes a showcase of performances, often with untrained musicians, culminating with the

atmosphere of a fast-food-style "Happy Meal" substituting for sacrifice, humility and silence....

It is...critical that our seminaries and institutions of higher education offer the truths of the Catholic Church. Philosophy and theology, not flash topics such as feminism, liberation theology, Celtic spirituality, creation theology or even vegetarianism, must form the central subjects of study.... No instruction in doctrine has meant a whole generation floundering.

The lack of real knowledge about the faith makes it difficult for many Catholics to defend themselves against one of the most prevalent charges launched against us: that we are unthinking, blind sheep—vaguely irrational and therefore proper objects of suspicion. Regardless of our professions and sometimes even advanced degrees and experience, we fear being ticked down a notch at work. We're afraid, maybe, to say that we're Catholic because we'll be known as one of *those* types: smart and capable, yes, but also into ephemeral, unrealistic superstition. Is it that we fear being labeled as somehow unworthy of promotion? "She's aces, sure, but she's into that Catholic stuff," we might imagine our supervisors saying over their conference room coffee. "Can we trust that she'll keep that stuff out of the project?"

Members of our generation report that we didn't even know about the Catholic heritage of intellectual and spiritual achievement until our thirties or later. Our religious education and experience did not nearly match the level of our professional education and experience, leaving our minds well-developed in our secular disciplines but ignorant of our faith. Many times, ours are impoverished hearts and souls. Too many of us, for instance, don't know what happens during the consecration. This startling fact was widely reported several years ago when a national survey found that many, even most Catholics, do not believe in the Real Presence of Christ in the Eucharist. We can ask, though, whether it's that we don't believe in the Real Presence or that we just were never taught the word *transubstantiation*?

As we realize how much we don't know, many of us are flocking to adult education classes in our parishes or even going for master's degrees in religion, theology, or Scripture after we've finished Ph.D.s, passed the bar or gone well beyond our social work, teaching or accounting degrees, licenses and certifications.

Don from Maryland realized his religious education had stood still while his secular or professional training advanced.

> Basically, it occurred to me that my faith and understanding of the Catholic Church had never matured. I left the Church as a young person and my catechism was frozen in time. I evolved as a person and an adult, but my faith remained mired in childish views and guilt-laden rules. The old verse that goes "when I was a child, I spoke as a child, thought as a child and acted like a child" was still true about my own level of understanding of faith and religion. My return to the faith community was really as simple as updating my catechism and dogma to coincide with my chronological age.

How does this desire to learn occur if our past education in Catholicism was so poor? Apparently, it happens in many ways, which we will explore in some detail later when we see how members of our generation are finally drifting back to the Church. For now, a brief answer seems to be serendipity (or a guardian angel's nudge) and the *Catechism of the Catholic Church*, which was published in an English translation in 1994.

Susan from Missouri writes that the same day she read our call for stories in *St. Anthony Messenger*, she also began to read the *Catechism*:

> And what a discovery and blessing for me! This book is explaining every aspect of the Catholic faith in easy-to-read language and in sufficient detail that hopefully when I finish reading it, it will give me a greater knowledge and appreciation for my faith which I have sorely been lacking throughout my entire life.
>
> I always continued to go to Mass every Sunday even though my understanding of the faith was so weak. It was a fragile faith, and I am hoping that by reading the *Catechism* my faith will deepen and become more enriched.

Apparently the *Catechism* has been a lifesaver and a starting point for many members of our generation of Catholics. To tell just one story from among several, Bob is in his late forties from upstate New York. As a twenty-year-old Episcopalian engaged to a Catholic, Bob took instructions to become a Catholic from an elderly priest who used the *Baltimore Catechism*. "Thank God for the new *Catechism*," he writes. "Whenever I asked this priest [almost 30 years ago], 'How do you know this?' he responded, 'It's a matter of faith.' Thank God for grace and spiritual gifts to feed one's faith."

What Bob seems to be saying is that, for us, learning about Catholicism is not simply memorizing tenets of the faith as our parents and grandparents did. We want to understand, feel and live our Catholic faith. We want to make it our own in a personal way.

It's interesting to note, however, that the call for a faith that is both learned in the head and felt in the heart has been echoing through the two thousand years of the Church's life. For example, in 1939 E.I. Watkin wrote *The Catholic Centre* (New York: Sheed & Ward), in which he stressed how absolutely critical it is for adult Catholics not only to know about our faith, but to live it.

> A sufficient Catholic education, which imparts a living organic and interior knowledge of the Catholic religion is now literally a matter of life or death. The Catholic today as he grows out of his childish acceptance must either go in to an interior vision of Catholic truth or go out of the Church....Come in or go out. You cannot stay on the surface. There is no foothold left there (page 54).

Although many older Catholics merely memorized the *Baltimore Catechism* and were left with an eighth-grade knowledge of their religion, others pursued further reading and study on their own and through parish study groups. Our generation, however, faces a new problem. It can no longer be taken for granted that young adult Catholics even know the fundamental facts of Catholicism. As has been noted above, those who taught us at times presumed that we already knew the basics and focused instead on teaching us to live out what we did not yet know.

The good news in all this is that some in our generation are enthusiastically discovering and embracing the Church's history and rich heritage. Veronica, a twenty-nine-year-old woman from Pennsylvania, recalls with excitement her passage from an uninformed faith that never really took root in her mind or soul to her own reading years later. Books finally introduced her to Catholic treasures she never even knew existed.

> I was born and raised a Catholic and when I was a child I had the faith of a child. I attended CCD classes but cannot tell you one thing I learned there. I made my Confirmation not really knowing what it was all about. In short, I fell away from the Church and lost my faith. I even agreed with others who downgraded the Church when I didn't even know anything about it.
>
> Now that I am a mother of two children, I have started to rediscover my faith through self-education. It is a wonderful, mystical, ancient faith. I didn't even know we were the first Church! Imagine that. I knew nothing.
>
> I feel the Church shouldn't assume her people know about her. They should teach, teach, teach. They should teach in catechism the basics of our faith. I'm so sorry this wasn't done with me. It could have saved a lot of confusion. I'm thankful that I'm learning to love my faith now, on my own. I am now starting to attend Mass again weekly, too.

Perhaps the message here is that if we learn about our faith— the events, heroes and villains, victories and defeats, doctrine and searching, faith and understanding—with honesty, sincerity and Veronica's sense of adventure, then we will be able to take the best from our past to help clarify our present and improve our future.

Riding the Stormy Seas of Vatican II

Our generation grew up at a time that was turbulent on all fronts: political, religious and social. Catholics were not only dealing with the changes Vatican II brought to the Church, but with the cataclysmic moments and movements hammering at the center of a world that seemed so solid. Martin from Pennsylvania tells his story:

> Born in 1956, I went to parochial school like all my cousins and a lot of my neighbors. It was that swirling time of Vatican II, but we were just out there in the American "wasteland," the sons and daughters of the sons and daughters of peasants who left Eastern Europe to come work in the coal mines of Pennsylvania. Vatican II came down to us in a muddle. We were too busy watching TV to think. World figures kept getting assassinated. It looked like nuclear war could happen any day.

Everyone and everything, it seemed, was adrift—including those handing on the faith. Looking back to the 1960's and 1970's, those of us who were growing up in the midst of the chaos can now begin to see and understand what happened. Our parents and teachers often unwittingly transferred their own creeping disaffection or disorientiation to us, their children and students, even as they struggled with the Church's changes themselves.

Moreover, the older members of our generation were raised in two Churches and some did not feel comfortable in either. Those who left the pre-Vatican II Church have now come back to a Church they don't recognize. Research bears this out. Williams and Davidson studied three groups of Catholics: those born before 1940, those born between 1941 and 1960, and those born between 1961 and 1976. They found that the middle group, who often identify themselves as raised in two Churches in their voices and stories for this book and elsewhere, were the "most conflicted" ("Catholic Conceptions of Faith," page 278).

The voice of a member of this conflicted middle group can give life to statistics. Kevin is a communications consultant and writer from Ontario who finds himself looking at his life and the Church in a detached way. He is still struggling to make sense of the changes that have accompanied his religious journey since he was baptized as a baby in 1952.

Try as I might, it's hard not to feel like an anthropologist, a nonparticipant observer, someone watching with detachment. There but not really there. In a strange way, this feeling captures something basic in my relationship with the institution of the Church for the past two decades. Often an observer, rarely have I felt a sense of belonging. Perhaps this is the "lostness" of my generation—those of us caught in the worst of both worlds. We have an overwhelmingly powerful childhood recollection of a fixed universe, where the Church and our parochial schools loomed large, where the priests and nuns (and there were always lots of them) made sure that right and wrong were unambiguously clear. Over and over they would reinforce the conviction that only Catholics were right. And we would do all we could, following their advice, not to make friends of Protestants. Fire and brimstone rained down on us in the form of thunderous pronouncements and accusations from the pulpit. "You! Creeping late like that. And late last week, too!" I remember looking around to discover, with aching fear, that he was pointing not at one of us school kids between the ages of five and eleven, but at someone who was older than my mother and was blushing, if not crying into a handkerchief.

Kevin reports that his experience of the pre-Vatican II Church frightened him, yet grounded him, too. Catholic things seemed clear-cut before the Council, many of our generation say. They say that the changes of Vatican II felt like a rug being pulled out from under them. They were initiated as children into a Church that was no longer around in their adult years.

Against that certainty crashed the shocking confusion of the early years of the post-conciliar Church. Nuns who had taught us for years suddenly appeared in what looked like nurse's uniforms. Some were angry and embarrassed. More threatening than these strange emotions was the shocking first glimpse of their hair, and their legs, once hidden under yards of thick black fabric.

And the Mass in English! Surely this had to be some lesser form of sacrament. Out with the chant and in come the guitars and the novelty of the folk-mass. I remember the local priests communicating a sort of benign tolerance, a sense that this unfortunate "blip" would soon be taken care of, that they were only going along with it because the bishop said so; because no one wants to go against the Holy Father himself, God bless him; and that after this weird modernist experiment fails, everything will return to the way it was always intended to be.

Except this "blip" endured.

What happened to the generation growing up Catholic around Vatican II, then, was complicated. Some people were glad to see the rigorism of the pre-Vatican II Church go and found the changes exciting and liberating. Others felt secure in the Church of the 1950's and found the changes disconcerting. Many embraced the opening up of the Vatican II Church and yet still felt uncomfortable with the quick pace of changes that were not always carefully or pastorally explained. This mix of excitement and confusion was particularly acute when we felt we were unlearning what we had been taught just a few years before.

Don captures our generation's feelings of being set adrift after being on seemingly solid ground. He recently rejoined the Church after twenty-five years and titles his story, "The Second Resurrection." Like others of us, Don describes himself as caught between two generations: Born just before Vatican II, he was raised and educated in the Council's aftermath.

My initial Catholic upbringing in the late fifties and early sixties was in a largely Catholic, coal-mining, blue-collar, small-town parochial grade school staffed by the Sisters of Saint Joseph. I received my first Holy Communion in a pre-Vatican II ceremony but was confirmed in a post-Vatican II event. Many adults as well as clergy were reacting to the multiple changes brought about by that [Council]. Their contempt and confusion was being subliminally expressed to students like me.

It was probably this post-Vatican II self-doubt and unrest that planted the seeds of discontent in my young Catholic faith. Dogma that I was told was absolutely true yesterday was suddenly changed or dismissed today. Couple this religious confusion with the vagaries of youthful adolescence and the disassociation began.

I was enrolled in a Catholic high school in a town that

housed a dichotomy of religious instructors. The principal was an older gentleman who embraced old order, history and tradition while the younger priests and nuns looked to the revised Church with enthusiasm and joy. However, the disparity was evident....

Most Catholics in our generation have absorbed the fruits of the Council. While some older Catholics may genuinely desire a return to the Church before the Council, and while some younger Catholics see the pre-Vatican II Church as something of a golden era, those of our generation who have some affiliation with today's Church are relatively comfortable there, even while they recognize its weaknesses.

Cheryl, a woman in her forties from California, embraced the "God is love" emphasis. Unlike other members of our generation, she was not turned off by the more nurturing, affective approach to the Church which sometimes accompanied Vatican II changes and is often derided as a Catholicism focused on "Jesus-as-a-warm-fuzzy." "God is good. God is love," she writes. "Those words stirred in me a longing I thought had died or was so deeply buried I would never again have God with me."

Cheryl began her drift from the Church when she started college in 1967. That was around the time the Vatican II changes were being implemented with various degrees of success and the United States was just about to step into some of its most turbulent years with Vietnam and Watergate. Thinking about her experiences now, Cheryl looks back with an understanding expressed in terms that reflect several decades of research into the links between spirituality and psychology.

> While many students leave the Church to explore other philosophies or paths, I left because I could no longer cope with a profound sense of failure or shame.
>
> My education in the faith was a CCD [Confraternity of Christian Doctrine] class for First Communion and four years of CCD classes while in high school. Our family faith was close to nonexistence. A child of an excommunicated, remarried mother, I was sent to Mass or went on my own. I listened to priests who concentrated on letting us know

how sinful we were and what a disappointment to God—
all of the time. As a teenager, shy and with low self-
esteem, Confession was painful and never felt like a
reconciliation that we now have. I was never taught about
the infinite forgiveness of God. To me, committing the
same sin was unforgivable. I was a failure and in some
cases I was ashamed of my sins.

Going to Communion? I was taught only Communion
after immediate Confession. So a vicious circle [followed]
that caused more guilt and sense of failure than love. I
remember always a sense of isolation. Youth ministry and
contact with other young Catholics was not part of my
Church parish. I talked to no one, no one talked to me
about spirituality and God's love.

It just seemed that I no longer could stand a conscience
and a God (Church) constantly making me feel worthless.
When I no longer had what seemed like "Big Daddy" (the
Church) constantly telling me I was a disappointment, I
was able to feel more normal.

Spiritual Surfing

The 1960's and the increased openness of the Vatican II
Church has led to a greater willingness to search for meaning
outside the Church as well as within it. This wandering can be
both exhilarating and disconcerting. For some of us it's a
process of touch and go as we find a place in a changing
Church. After drifting away from the pre-Vatican II Church of
his 1950's childhood, Kevin writes of finding himself wandering
into a new-style Church during a penance service in the 1980's:

> The church is fan-shaped inside, built according to, rather
> than adapted to, the requirements of the new liturgy.
> There's even carpet on the floor. And so much light. I
> discover I have walked into some form of penitential
> service. I'm lost. There is no accusation, no threat, just a
> gentle invitation to reflect on the choices we make. Then,
> another type of choice is offered. We can go into the
> church hall to receive a collective form of absolution, or we
> can line up and wait our turn for the reconciliation room.
> I have no idea what happens in a reconciliation room,

but I discover that I am equally determined to find out. My determination and terror fight with each other as I join the lineup, my heart thumping and palms oozing perspiration. The door opens. It's my turn and I'm genuinely flustered. I lost my pretense somewhere back in the lineup and I feel an aching need to be here, even if I don't fully understand why.

I have no idea what the right words are. I only know my neediness and my confusion. Words race around my head and sprint away in confused embarrassment.

The young priest, like me probably in his early thirties, is totally collected and comfortable with fear and silence. We finally talk, or rather I babble and he listens. He says something about acceptance and forgiving as an adult those things that still grip us years later because of the powerful way we were taught so long ago. We have to allow our adult sense of compassion and our child-born faith to catch up with each other. I start to cry. He gives me a tissue and his blessing and I feel, not exhilarated, certainly not "born again," not even fully aware, just strangely and quietly unburdened.

Kevin returned to the same church for Mass later that week only to feel left out by the regular parishioners, unfamiliar music and a distracted priest. "Coming home is never the direct, uncomplicated journey we long for," Kevin recalls, reflecting his sad disappointment after a good experience of reconciliation. "And so it goes for over a decade, little flickers of hope and discovery in a prairie landscape of spiritual homelessness."

Kevin relates a common experience of our generation: a confused feeling of some sorrow, guilt or remorse because we've been drifting. We try to make up for our years away from the Church now by taking classes or living the faith more openly and overtly by participating in programs, especially social justice activities.

But should our generation feel guilty about lost time and our experiences of spiritual surfing? Psychologists and sociologists say the answer is, basically, no. Looking at the experiences of many people in our generation especially, we can see a natural pattern. Our early twenties, for most of us, were a time of searching, stretching and settling into an adult life. Our religious development is part of this process. Spiritual directors often advise that wherever our life is, our prayer life will be there, too. If we're unsettled in a career path or just living frenetically, our spiritual life will also feel distracted, searching and unsettled.

This is not meant to be an excuse, but it is an explanation. And that explanation may help our generation in two ways. First, we might not have cause to feel *crushing* guilt about ignoring our faith for a while. Even Saint Francis and Saint Augustine encountered a time of spiritual drift. We can lament lost time, but we don't have to die spiritually because of it. Second, the spiritual journey explanation might also help us to understand that struggling with our faith as young adults— even abandoning our faith for a time—may in fact be part of our path as we embrace our Catholic heritage as adults.

Learning that it was okay to struggle with her growth in faith comforted Susan, a magazine reporter in her mid-twenties:

> Recently, while attending a conference for work, I learned about the stages of faith development. I was totally blown away. All this time I thought I was being an awful Catholic and in all actuality, my actions and feelings were normal. I attended Catholic schools from grade school through college, and this was the first I had ever heard about different stages of faith development. I find it really unfortunate that no one ever explained this to me. I also found it very interesting, though, that my own faith was strengthened by something that I still wouldn't know [about] if it wasn't for work sending me to that convention. I wonder how many other people my age feel unnecessarily alienated from the Church as I did.
>
> Seeing the different stages of faith development and what they encompass gave me a new appreciation for the difficulties the Church faces in ministering to the faithful on so many different faith levels. Not to mention that people can always be jumping from one stage to another.
>
> If only I had known sooner.

It seems important to take some time here to understand the stages of faith development in young adults. The summary that follows might put our generation's experience of drifting away from the Church into some context and offer hope for the possibilities of drifting back. Some of the most important work on the spiritual tasks of young adulthood has been done by James W. Fowler, Sharon Parks, Patrick H. McNamara and Wade Clark Roof. Research like theirs formed a key part of the background, planning and writing of the bishops' 1997 statement on young adult ministry, *Sons and Daughters of the Light*. Their findings may be as comforting and enlightening to you as they were to Susan and me.

James W. Fowler identified our young adult years as a transition stage in spiritual development in *Stages of Faith: The Psychology of Human Development and the Quest for Meaning* and *Becoming Adult, Becoming Christian: Adult Development and Christian Faith*. Particularly in *Becoming Adult, Becoming Christian*, Fowler found that young adults are in a process of finding a personal and professional vocation within a religious context that gives meaning to the totality of their lives. He spoke of vocation not in the narrow sense of priesthood or membership in a religious order, but in the broadest sense of seeing our lives through a religious prism. Such a viewpoint, he concluded, is what gives meaning to the lives of adult Christians.

Sharon Parks took Fowler's work and applied it more specifically to young adults. For her study, *The Critical Years: The Young Adult Search for a Faith to Live By*, especially pages 73-106, Parks surveyed young adults across the country. She identified young adulthood as a key stage on the path to mature adulthood. It was not "merely transitional," to use her evocative phrases, but a key period full of both "promise and vulnerability" in which we forge our identities on the "threshold of adulthood." Building on Fowler's findings, she saw young adulthood as a time when we choose for ourselves to accept or reject a religious tradition that was offered to us as children, but against which we might have naturally rebelled as teenagers or college students.

At bottom, Parks identifies young adulthood as a period of searching for spiritual wholeness. As she put it, "ambivalence, wariness, exploration, and tentativeness are the warp and woof of the tapestry of faith woven in the young adult era" (page 82). As young adults, especially fresh out of college, we idealistically try to conquer the world, often to find ourselves overwhelmed by the crushing magnitude and particulars of an impossible dream. Over time, we move from ideals to understanding that we must be pragmatic. Sometimes as a result of this realization we turn sour and disillusioned; we might abandon our ideals. The path to mature adulthood, Parks maintains, is when we can strike a balance between pragmatism and idealism. Then we have learned how to take actions and the responsibility for those actions, including the rejection or acceptance of our Catholicism on adult terms.

Many members of our generation of Catholics have been engaged in this kind of spiritual search, whether through Protestant evangelical churches, New Age movements, Eastern religions with their emphasis on meditation, or the spirituality of Twelve-Step programs.

Some of us make up our own religious life, much as we would make a tapestry. Elizabeth from Ohio, along with her husband and their three sons, shopped around and picked from a variety of the mainstream faiths that they shared with their housemates.

> We tried various churches, but we didn't seem to fit in and eventually it was easier to just not go. I never did try out the Catholic Church. I just never thought that I'd go back, though I did go to Midnight Mass every Christmas with my family but more as a family tradition than a worship service....
>
> One of our housemates was from a Jewish tradition, and we celebrated the Sabbath, Hannukah and Passover with her. I could see that the boys enjoyed these celebrations so we continued to celebrate them when we moved, but I felt the need to get the boys (and myself) involved in a Christian church.
>
> When he was young, my husband attended the United Church of Christ. There was one nearby so we decided to

try going there. I was hoping that my husband would get involved, but after attending a few times he told me he didn't need to attend an organized church to be a good Christian so he wasn't going to go anymore. The boys enjoyed it (they liked the pastor) so we continued to go even though I felt dissatisfied.

People like Elizabeth are looking for a way to synthesize a great deal of religious information and choices into a system that both makes sense and gives meaning to our existence as individuals. But while it is a natural part of the spiritual journey, our generation's experience of Church makes it peculiarly difficult. Don, the Maryland man who rejoined the Church, describes his experiences of drifting:

> When I talked to a lot of practicing Catholics and ex-Catholics, I still encountered a lot of disgust or disagreement regarding what it was to be a Catholic in the 1980's. There were so many splintered factions, it was hard to tell what the true Catholic Church was or even what it stood for. I really felt lost.

We are trying to find our own religious identity and vocation; we don't want it imposed on us. When this natural psychological and spiritual stage was set amid the promise and confusion of Vatican II, the result was the proverbial formula for disaster. All some of us could do, it seems, was tread water for a while.

This Is *Not* Our Parents' Catholicism

Another reason why our generation may have drifted away from the Church is that the Catholicism practiced by our parents' generation and taught to some of us in pre-Vatican II parochial school or CCD classes seems divorced from our current faith experiences and spiritual desires. Of course, we're not talking here about unchangeable principles of the faith, but rather about how our devotion to our faith is discussed, exercised and understood. The core beliefs of our Catholicism are the core beliefs of our parents' Catholicism and of the

Catholicism of two millennia of our ancestors. But the feeling, the practice, the culture of our Catholicism is certainly not the feeling, practice and culture of our parents' Catholicism.

Theresa's experiences offer us a wonderful, enlightening illustration of this dichotomy. She came to realize that how we practice our Catholic faith today is not always like our parents' practice of Catholicism or our own childhood devotions. Now in her mid-thirties, Theresa grew up in western New York state as an everyday good Catholic kid.

> When I made my First Communion at the age of six, nobody would have ever thought that I would eventually stray from the Church. I was so proud and loved God so much. I would sing at the top of my lungs. As a child, I loved everything about being Catholic. I loved to pray and talk to God. I went to Confession, Communion and special Masses.

Interestingly, it was an experience at Confession that led Theresa away from the Church. But it wasn't the stereotypical story we've all heard: "I-got-thrown-out-of-the-confessional-and-I'll-never-go-back-to-those-hypocritical-jerks-again!" In fact, it was a post-Vatican II experience of the personal invitation to reconciliation that made her react against her parents' pre-Vatican II sense of the duty, even the burden to confess.

> When I was about seventeen years old [in the late 1970's], my parents would force us to go to Confession monthly. I felt, "Why should I go to Confession when I do nothing wrong?" During Confession, the priest asked me what I had to confess. I told him that my parents had forced me to come to Confession. He told me [that], at my age, my parents should not force me to go to Church or Confession. He stated that when I was ready I would go on my own.
>
> I left the confessional and went to my seat next to my mother. She asked me why I wasn't saying my penance and I told her what Father told me. She was very mad....
>
> It was at that time that I totally left the Catholic Church. I still considered myself Catholic, but did not practice. I

only went to funerals and weddings. I never went to Christmas, Easter, or any other Masses. I had nothing religious in my life. This broke my parents' heart.

It's not always this easy to get ahold of the dichotomy between, on the one hand, our parents' Catholicism and the devotions taught to some of us educated in the late 1950's and 1960's, and on the other hand the post-Vatican II experience of Catholicism. Elizabeth remembers a certain comfort in her first Holy Communion in a pre-Vatican II Mass, even if she didn't understand what was going on until the Mass switched to English a few years later.

> When I made my first Communion in the second grade I can remember being confused and not sure what was going on, but it was something we were supposed to do and not question. Mass was still in Latin then. My little missal was full of unfamiliar words. It wasn't too long after that when the Mass went to English. It was much easier for a little girl to understand, but some of the mystery was gone. One thing I especially remember and miss is the ringing of the bells at certain times during the Mass.

Some members of our generation remember a sense of mystery from the "old" Mass even while admitting they were lost during its celebration. But it's still hard to compare our parents' clear, solid "brand" of Catholicism with our own. Why? Because it's hard to label a "brand" of post-Vatican II Catholicism. Again, young adult Catholics often share a feeling that we drifted away from one Church with no firm idea of the Church we're trying to return to or create anew.

Let's try, however, to put our practice or "brand" of Catholicism in context. Along with Williams' and Davidson's article "Catholic Conceptions of Faith," we'll draw here on two key studies of the post-Vatican II experience and exercise of faith. The first, Wade Clark Roof's *A Generation of Seekers*, looked at people of different faiths born between 1946 and 1964, or part of our generation of Catholics. Although Catholicism and Vatican II were not major areas of analysis, *A Generation of*

Seekers still points the way to general trends in the religious experiences and practices of Americans during the last several decades.

In speaking of faithful people in general, not just Catholics, Roof noted a pattern: Those who drifted away from formal religion and an institutional affiliation with a Church or synagogue but have returned now frequently "stress the psychological aspects of faith."

> One thing they look for in shopping around for a congregation is an emphasis on "feeling" religion, on bringing the experiential and belief dimensions of faith into a vital balance. Many of them never abandoned their beliefs, but often the beliefs seem disjointed from their life experiences. Congregations where the atmosphere helps to bring these two—belief and experience—into some meaningful whole are more likely to capture their loyalties.... A psychological language of "choices" and "needs" replaces older-style religious obligations as a basis for getting involved in a congregation. Much of the shopping around occurs in an attempt to find a match between personal needs and institutional styles. For many of them, the search begins with the assumption that getting your needs met in a congregation will *not* be easy—58% see most churches and synagogues as having lost the real spiritual part of religion (*A Generation of Seekers*, page 192).

Our parents and teachers were raised in a Catholic world marked by the Council of Trent which in the 1500's shored up the walls of Catholicism that had been nibbled—in some cases, blown—away by the Protestant Reformation. For several hundred years, an institutional focus dominated Catholicism, a sort of "top-down" Catholicism which emphasized authority and obedience. The piety that often resulted was highly personal—what some of us may remember as our grandparents whispering the rosary during Mass instead of actively participating in the communal celebration of the Eucharist as we were urged to do in the 1970's and 1980's. But even personal devotions were chosen from among accepted Catholic practices.

A Catholic culture within the broader, mainstream society also tended to reinforce high-profile practices such as novenas, the Stations of the Cross and no-meat Fridays.

What emerged after Vatican II, however, was a greater focus on individual spirituality and less on an institutional or formal affiliation with the Catholic Church. As Roof concluded:

> Boomers see religion in somewhat different ways than their parents did—with a greater concern for spiritual quest, for connectedness and unity, and for a vision that encompasses body and spirit, the material as well as the immaterial.... For many, maybe even the majority of Boomers today, personal faith and spirituality seem somehow disconnected from many of the older institutional religious forms (*A Generation of Seekers*, pages 26, 30).

These findings are reflected in the second study we'll consider. In 1992, Patrick H. McNamara published *Conscience First, Tradition Second: A Study of Young American Catholics*. McNamara's findings came from a study in which he interviewed every graduating senior from an urban Catholic high school in New Mexico from 1977 to 1989. He surveyed over two thousand graduates and then met up with more than fifty of them for a follow-up survey about a decade after they graduated to measure their thoughts on Catholicism over time.

These high school seniors, when interviewed a decade after their graduation, indicated they were more interested in their individual spirituality as opposed to formal ties with the institutional Church. McNamara's study also identified a decline of what he called pre-Vatican II "devotional Catholicism" since Vatican II. His respondents said they felt distanced from their parents' traditions. We might add that many of us born later and later after Vatican II have grown increasingly ignorant of that tradition, as well. Ironically, McNamara found that devotional Catholicism often imparted a sense of identity and security, the loss of which is frequently reported by younger Catholics in the 1970's and 1980's.

Furthermore, the more McNamara's young Catholic respondents became assimilated into a mainstream American culture that was less Catholic, the more they became alienated from what little Catholic identity was imparted in their post-Vatican II Catholic high school experience. Although this trend has been noted by sociologists and observers of previous generations, it may be more true of our generation since we had virtually none of the Catholic culture with which our parents grew up. Once again, we were set adrift.

In what other ways does the dichotomy between our parents' institutional "brand" of Catholicism and our generation's more shifting, unsettled experience play out as we drift away from and back toward the Church? One measure might be self-identification as Catholics. How do we young adults identify ourselves as Catholics?

Many people we know in our families, networks of friends and at work identify themselves as Catholics even though they don't go to Mass or only go to church for weddings and funerals. Roof found that eighty-five percent of Baby-Boom Catholics who were surveyed reported their belief that a Catholic can be considered a good Catholic without attending Mass on Sunday. Nearly ninety percent said you can be a good Catholic even if you don't put money in the collection basket (*A Generation of Seekers*, pages 232-233). In another survey, sixty-three percent of Catholics born in our parents' and grandparents' generations (between 1910 and 1940) reported that they went to Mass once a week or more while just twenty-four percent of Catholics born in the 1960's and 1970's could say the same thing (*Laity: American and Catholic*, page 76).

McNamara's study found similar results among teenagers who then became young adults in the 1980's and 1990's. In the graduating class of 1989, only half reported that they went to Mass every Sunday while another twenty-five percent said they never attend Mass or go only a few times each year. Asked if religion was important in their lives, half as many responded yes at the end of the survey period in the late 1980's than had responded yes a decade before. As to their parish involvement, over fifty percent of the 1989 graduating class said that they had little or no interest in participating in their parish's activities. Less than one in five even described themselves as "active."

But there are other signs that give some hope and reason

for optimism. True, our experience of Catholicism is quite different from that of our parents. Still, that doesn't mean our generation of Catholics hasn't been searching for religious meaning in the 1980's and 1990's. The wave of popular interest in that conglomeration of spiritual practices and fads collectively called the New Age may be good news. After all, only hungry people search for food.

What does our generation want from religious experiences? Many of us indicate in surveys that we want to live our faith through action in the world. Roof contrasted traditional exercises of Mass attendance and financial contributions with social justice to make this point. Among Catholics, Roof found "overwhelming support for a social justice commitment. Only nineteen percent say that a person can be a good Catholic *without* being concerned about the poor" (*A Generation of Seekers*, page 232, emphasis added). It's clear, then, that we want an activist faith where our Monday-to-Saturday lives are directly connected with what we do and hear preached on Sunday. Put bluntly, we're working in soup kitchens more than we're kneeling in pews.

Finally, while our generation has tended to be critical of the Church, young adult minister John Roberto notes that our criticism must be viewed properly. In an article with the provocative title, "Is Our Church Losing the Next Generation of Catholics?" (published in *American Catholic Identity: Essays in an Age of Change*, pages 167-77), Roberto argued that critical reflection of faith during young adulthood reflects real concern and interest in Catholicism. Would we complain about something we didn't care about? Our critical approach to the Church and all things religious represents a balanced search for ideals and pragmatic results. Roberto identifies this as a "searching style of faith," which leads to personal growth. "We normally call this adult faith—the faith of convictions, the faith that is internalized and owned," he writes.

It's the faith that those who have been drifting are now returning to embrace.

PART TWO

Drifting Back

As often as we meet people our age who have drifted away from the Church, it seems that more frequently members of our generation have been starting to drift back to the Church. Some may not have returned fully yet, but are on their way. Still others may remain far away, but that doesn't mean they have completely ruled out the possibility of taking a few steps back. It may be that something Catholic was planted deep within us, even if we rebelled against it, that continues to call us home.

How is our generation coming home? Some of those who return indicate that once they've returned or have started on a path back to the Church, they feel they've come back to a God who was waiting all along and to a Church that was finding itself again after some stormy years. Many describe a time when they realized they were on a pilgrim's journey that strayed from the Church, but inevitably is leading back home. That return path takes many forms, but there are some common components.

Pilgrims' Feet

Members of our generation are pilgrims, just like anyone else on a religious journey. We're always on our way, stumbling and bumbling sometimes, other times striding with ease. Like Chaucer's pilgrims headed toward Canterbury, we're not at our destination yet, but we're talking, laughing, thinking and telling our stories as we go along. Drifting back, we find, is a process.

Some members of our generation say we're comfortable with the concept of process, maybe because we grew up with the language of "becoming" instead of "being" from our psychology textbooks. Perhaps it's because we're used to change. Unsteady economic conditions taught us that our lives will change in terms of careers, particular jobs within a career and places to live far more than those who lived in the earlier part of this century. Many of our parents worked for the same company and lived in the same house for their entire married lives. We, on the other hand, have become more accustomed to moving around.

Now, let's link this acceptance of change to our spiritual lives. Some in our generation say that drifting amid change—or spiritual surfing, as we called it earlier—is in fact an integral, instructive and potentially rich part of our pilgrim's path back to the Catholic Church.

The return home makes some of us, children of the most technologically advanced era in history, feel like we're pieces of e-mail: distinct and individual messages floating around in religious cyberspace. In the words of Kevin, a communications consultant:

> [We] form a kind of global "virtual" community. We connect from time to time, creating a loose network of involvement. A short, often intense, but just as often casual and conversational exchange after long periods of noncommunication. Even so, this casual "network" remains, quietly humming away in the background. It's a little like having a personal version of the Internet—that loose global network of sources of information that connect, but only when called upon, and often in rather surprising ways. Start searching for one topic on the net and you end up somewhere else altogether. But in this case, it's not bits and bytes of information, but encouragement, support, challenge and clearly a lot of prayer.

Kevin continues the story of his pilgrim's journey as he slowly drifted back home to the Catholic Church:

> We all long for home, believing it takes the form of an actual place, while all along we intuit, deep down, that it is more a different kind of experience, more of an awareness and an attitude than a building.

He asked around for a good parish, and two friends pointed to the same suburban parish, which for him

...is becoming home in its own way. This is where a prayerful liturgy, inspired preaching, a great inclusiveness—and my neediness—sustain me, week after week. And week after week I feel the need to return. I'm not officially "signed up" yet, so I am still somewhat of a guest. But I'm certainly more than a nonparticipant observer. I have started working for their food bank program. These are externals. The real movement lies within, in a changing attitude, a deepening faith, and a whole new sense of acceptance. It is all too easy to call this the experience of growing up. We can lose something by trying to describe it, to capture it definitively in words. Whatever "this" is, it is the result of years of anguished search....

Mine is a small step, one that acknowledges how difficult it is to make your way back to something that you were never really a part of in the first place. Years of watching from the sidelines sharpen your protective instincts and your need to keep your distance, even when others are clearly reaching out. And reaching out they are, if we make the effort to notice.

This man speaks eloquently for those who hankered to return home, even if it took a long time to reconnect. Others, however, completely shut out any connection to the Church for many years. Now, however, reflecting on our journeys, some of us begin to realize that we were drifting away, and then back, without even knowing it. The Church remained a lighthouse for the journey, whether we cared to notice or not.

Theresa is typical. She had a good education, including a master's degree in administration, and a solid career as a registered nurse. She left the Church around the time of her high school graduation, but years later she realized something was missing in her life. Finally, at the age of thirty-two, Theresa came to a realization that began with feelings of emptiness.

I had a very well-paying job, a sports car, my own house and a lot of friends. But something was missing. I felt very low. My friend who is a psychologist could not figure it out. I had not lost anything in my life. Why was I acting depressed? She encouraged me to go to a support group for people with stress-related problems. I went and still felt a large void in my life. She suggested that I go on vacation, so I did. In November 1993, a friend and I went to Florida. I felt very uneasy during the vacation, like I could not relax. I spent hours on the beach. In fact one day my friend found me on the beach with the waves crashing over me. I tried desperately to figure out what was wrong with me.

Finally, one starlit night, I went out onto the beach. There was nobody on the beach, just me, the sand, the waves and the stars. I looked to Heaven and said, "God, please help me to change my life. I will do anything for you if only my life could get better." At that moment, I felt some peace. I had given my life back to God.

Back home, she changed jobs, entered a nurse practitioner's program and returned to Mass.

Every day became a new blessing from God. I found a church that I really loved. [St. Gregory's] became my healing place.... I started to go to church weekly, then I actually joined the parish (got my envelopes). I began going to church daily and then joined several groups at church. I was working full-time, going to school full-time, and still had time to devote to God. My life was becoming fulfilled.

Theresa, like many of our generation, hit bottom before she could reach out. In order to start coming back to the Church, she realizes now that she first had to realize what she was missing by being away. Although her story is not as extreme as others who report they reached out for God from the depths of clinical depression, broken families or substance abuse, she still felt the need for God as a lack of wholeness. On that starlit beach in Florida, Theresa realized that it came down to her and God in that personal relationship that seems so important for our confused, drifting generation.

Once back, Theresa became active in her parish,

contributing to its financial support and embracing its community outreach. She ended up as one of the founding members of her diocese's Young Adult Ministry, having found that "evangelization and helping others to find their way back to the Church was my mission in life." For now, she's tapping into her own experiences of drifting. Having found the religious meaning of her life, Theresa is now helping other pilgrims drift back:

> I had felt bad for leaving God, but as I look back on those years [I see that] God walked with me and held me when I needed it. He has lifted me up to help serve others. My journey with God has ripened as I discern my vocation to his call. I will forever help people like myself to begin their journey with God.
>
> God has found one of his lost sheep. I will help him find the others.

Pilgrims' feet walk many paths. Sometimes, as in the case of Theresa's current activities, it takes a "found" sheep to reassure others who are lost that there is hope and a home. Some discovered, ironically, that they bottomed out spiritually as they achieved success in their secular professions. Others relate that a shattering personal experience brought their lives up short and sent them back to their origins. Often, a single kindness, a welcome, a reconnection with God or a family tragedy can push us back onto the pilgrim's path. Many say that they were brought back by a good priest or nun who blew away sad, bitter or angry childhood memories of a frightening, maybe even mean, teacher or member of the clergy.

In the case of Don from Maryland, an energetic, enthusiastic, sincere young parish priest was a key factor in his decision to return:

> After experiencing the personal invitations of several friends, talking about the positive aspects of the Catholic faith, learning about the changes made in the past twenty-seven years, and seeing Father's faith in action, it compelled me to rejoin, and my wife to convert to the Catholic faith.

Often a combination of factors brings people to a church door after a time away. Don's story reminds us that drifting back is a process that requires time, readiness and welcoming hands. In addition, the goal of the process, returning to the Church, is often triggered by an emotional event. In Don's case, when he was forty-two in 1995, his mother was diagnosed with an inoperable brain tumor; she died of emphysema six weeks later. As he recounts his experience, he sees how her death allowed him to connect his past experiences with the Church with his current life and challenges.

> Just as Christ's death and resurrection brought about our salvation, so my mother's death brought about mine. Seeing the inner peace and acceptance of her imminent death and her faith that through death comes life brought back a flood of spiritual rekindling in me. It became important for me to ensure she was afforded every possible grace at this time. I wanted her to have Last Rites (now called Anointing of the Sick, I learned) and my [Protestant] wife noticed a level of reverence and connectivity heretofore not evidenced in our twenty-three years of marriage. It was at that time that my wife insisted, "You have got to get back to the Catholic faith where you belong."

Don and his wife were neighbors to a woman who turned out to be the coordinator of their parish's RCIA program. She was familiar with people who had questions and concerns about the Catholic Church. She invited Don and his wife to her parish. At first, they were apprehensive. But then they heard positive stories about the Church. The couple began to understand that they were labeling today's Church with yesterday's terms.

These pilgrim experiences include typical elements of drifting back to the Church that are repeated in the stories of many members of our generation.

Catch the Spirit!

Members of our generation also report that they were attracted to Protestant evangelical movements on their pilgrim paths. These evangelical liturgies and other activities sometimes called to them when they were ready to embrace religion as adults after a dry spell. Other times, evangelical enthusiasm pulled them away from Catholicism during high school or college. For some, the spirited Protestant celebrations filled a need that wasn't being addressed in Catholic parishes, even in the post-Vatican II wave of lively liturgies. For others, the Protestant emphasis on the Bible captured their intellectual interest, especially when they realized that their Protestant friends were far more well-versed in Sacred Scripture than they were. Moreover, at a time when the Catholic Church seemed to be stumbling and confused, the Protestant evangelicals offered a certainty that many longed for. They opened their arms wide. To eager, searching eyes, they offered little of the Catholic baggage carried from childhood.

The allure of the Protestant evangelical movement reached across the country during the 1970's and 1980's, especially when it became linked with politics and activism. The spirit-filled worship and the lack of institutional apparatus captured many disillusioned young Catholics. We were looking for something that we did not believe our Catholic heritage had given us even after Vatican II. We wanted action, inside the church building and outside, and we didn't think the Catholic Church was giving us what we craved.

This was the case with Jim, a thirty-three-year-old man from New Jersey. As a child, Jim dutifully went to Mass with his parents and sisters every Sunday. He also attended CCD through his Confirmation in the sixth grade. "I prayed in church and when I was worried about a test or some other problem," he writes. "We did not pray as a family, nor did we read the Bible in our home very much." In 1982 he went to college and continued to attend Mass where he "saw God Sunday morning and left him pretty much right there in the church."

But then, as a college freshman, Jim met up with a Protestant evangelical movement that turned him on in a way his Catholic upbringing never did.

A change started coming over my life, however, after I was

invited to a nondenominational Christian fellowship on campus. I attended the first meeting and was overwhelmed with the love and concern I noted from the people there. I belonged to other clubs on campus, but had not experienced anything like this.

We spent the first thirty minutes with guitar playing and singing songs praising God. Next, two people in front of the room took prayer requests (there were thirty to forty people in the room). Then they prayed for ten to fifteen minutes over those requests. This was very different from anything I had experienced before, but I was moved by it. For the last forty-five minutes we had someone lead a Bible study.

It was at a Christian Fellowship meeting that I first heard the Gospel! That Jesus died on the cross for my sins and through His death and resurrection my sins were forgiven and I had eternal life....I knew that Jesus died on the cross and rose on Easter morning. I believed that from my earliest days. However, I did not know the significance of it for me.

I had not been taught up until this point to nurture a personal relationship with Christ. I was amazed that growing up in the Catholic Church I had never heard this message before....I grew up in the Catholic Church, but yet did not have an understanding of the gospel. I believe there are many people in the Church who are still ignorant of the gospel.

Others came to the Protestants by a different path, one that was not linked with positive aspects of religion and spirituality. For some, the evangelical movement allowed them to "get back" at or "get even" with the Catholic Church, becoming a vehicle for their anger. Having abandoned Catholicism, for example, Martin dabbled in transcendental meditation, the spirituality of Alcoholics Anonymous, faith in reincarnation and even horoscopes. Then, he reports, the Protestant evangelicals' emphasis on the Bible and God's individual attention grabbed him when he was about thirty-five.

Something happened to me in 1991 or 1992. I started to read the Bible and come in contact with certain Protestant

Christians. I started to watch the "700 Club," prayed with Pat Robertson a couple of times. Something happened. The reality of Jesus came to me personally. I "accepted" Christ as my "personal Savior."... [Two years later, my mother and I] were both dunked, "rebaptized" in our good old friendly Calvinist Baptist Church. You may as well have called it "Friendly Baptist!" There was at least a little bit of something real about it. And in our baptism we were making a statement about our lives being committed to Jesus Christ, and Jesus Christ alone (and not the Blessed Mother, nor Saint Anthony, nor Saint Francis, nor Saint Therese of Lisieux, all "patrons" in our Catholic past).

Martin now sees his time with a fundamentalist, born-again church as part of his faith journey back to the Catholic Church even though, at the time, he even joined in Catholic bashing.

No way did I consider returning to the Roman Catholic Church at that time. From ex-Catholics, and plain old anti-Catholics, I learned that the Roman Church was in fact "the apostate Church," "the whore of Babylon" mentioned in Revelation 17 and 18. I tried to tell my Dad, a Catholic, of course, and a weekly communicant, who doesn't like to talk about God too much. We had arguments! And I argued with my aunt [a former nun]. The upshot was that my mother "took my side" and came with me to "Bible Church."

But there is another side of the story: a creeping disaffection with the Protestant evangelical movement. What happened after the music died? Were the externals meeting internal needs? Many answered no. They wanted more—and began to realize that the Catholic Church from which they drifted away held what they needed. They began to drift back.

Listen again to Teri. As a teenager in 1978, Teri attended a Christian rock concert:

[The lead singer] invited those who wanted to receive Christ to come forward. Most of the bleachers emptied as the young people came down the stairs. Not only the bleachers. So too my practice of Catholicism emptied. For the next three years I spent my energies and prayers

directed toward evangelical outreach. I would attend
various Christian concerts,...read fundamentalist tracts
detailing how close the Rapture was, attend mass baptisms
[at a local lake], and only listen to a local Christian Rock
radio station. I went through the motions of going to Mass,
but eagerly awaited Sunday nights to go to the "real"
Church service.

The fundamentalist evangelical meetings and Bible study
groups she attended began to grow enormously, moving from
the basement of an Episcopal church to a municipal auditorium.
When a permanent structure was being built, she and her
friends would gather on the concrete foundations under the
steel scaffolding. "No walls had been installed and so it was
rather a huge tent—a huge revival," she remembers.

But something important changed for Teri. The leader, as
was his custom, invited those who wanted to receive Jesus to
come forward.

As congregants applauded the newly saved (perhaps a
couple were signalling their approval of the band's newest
tune, too), the thought came, "This is not for you. This is
not where you belong." I walked out of the sanctuary and
have not had any desire to attend any service [there] since.
I had continued to go to morning Sunday Mass to placate
my parents and others, while attending [the evangelical
meeting] at night. Once I stopped going to [the evangelical
meeting] I continued to attend Sunday Mass. I really
didn't "feel" anything, but just continued in the habit of
Sunday Mass, as it was the Catholic way to go to church.

She was drifting back.

Other members of our generation were similarly captured
by the Protestants' emphasis on a personal God, on Scripture
and on social ties. But, at the same time that they welcomed
these religious practices that they hadn't experienced in their
Catholic upbringing, they also felt a nagging pull for something
more. This, in fact, is the story of Jean Marie, a woman we've
already met. She attended Mass and joined a Catholic Young
Adult Ministry but, she reports, she was turned off by the way
the members acted. As a result, she stopped attending Mass

again, as she had done before in college. Then Jean Marie began to date a Protestant,

> a man from another denomination who seemed to "walk the walk" which he talked. In his church, I learned to read the Bible as though it were addressed to me, personally. This made God "real" to me again and I attended every church service, Bible study and young adult function. The minister's wife invited me to their home for coffee, a family was assigned to "adopt" me and involved me in their family activities, and I surrounded myself with Christians who seemed to live what they believed. This is what I was looking for.

Jean Marie reports that these encounters were not her first experience of the Holy Spirit moving within her. The Protestant denomination that welcomed her in the 1980's tapped into a "felt" relationship with the Holy Spirit she had within Catholicism in the late 1970's. But this relationship was not followed up in her other Catholic religious experiences.

> At my confirmation in the tenth grade, I prayed to the Holy Spirit that if God was real, he must "hit me over the head" so I could know him without a doubt. The following year, I attended a Search where I received my first Bible and my hunger for God grew, along with the feeling that the Holy Spirit had become my "secret friend"; I felt secure in a deep part of myself, sensing his presence in me.

Despite her comfort with a highly "spiritual" experience of Christian faith among her Protestant friends, Jean Marie still felt that only by finding the missing piece of her Catholic past could she complete her religious picture. Jean Marie's guard was up. She began to search for some blend of her adult experience of the Protestant evangelical spirit with her childhood memories of a Catholic institutional grounding.

> But I longed for a sense of the sacred, the example of the saints, the Eucharist and the Blessed Mother. I was afraid of the apparent lack of authority and accountability in the Protestant churches. What would keep me from learning

and believing lies, or at least partial truths regarding God?

Was there such a thing as Catholic Christians, Catholics who loved God, who knew God (didn't just know about God) and lived their beliefs?

We hear a similar voice from Connecticut, where a 43-year-old woman named Diane writes that she, too, found her interest in the Christian faith sparked from outside Catholic circles. And while her spirit was captured, Diane's heart and mind told her she wanted something more than what the allure of this Christian denomination offered. She sensed she would find her answer right where she had started.

An encounter with Jehovah's Witnesses began Diane's drift back to Catholicism. Diane was raised Catholic and attended Mass with her mother while her father stayed home. She took CCD classes but doesn't remember anything at all from them. Although she sometimes skipped Mass during college, after graduation she made a special effort to attend every Sunday. She married, had three children in six years and settled into life as Mom.

> Then one day the doorbell rang. It was the Jehovah's Witnesses. Well, I am a friendly person and I love my God and, let's face it, I was an adult home all day long with three little kids. I could use someone to talk to. So I let them in and we read the Bible. They asked me if they could come back the next week. I said sure. So it went for weeks and weeks.

These Jehovah's Witnesses were showing Diane how little she knew about her own Catholic faith.

> I really enjoyed talking about my faith. I also found it fascinating how they interpreted the Bible. Of course, they were out to convert me, but I told them I was happy with my Catholic faith. So they challenged me. They asked me a lot of questions. They told me a lot of things about the history of the Catholic Church. I started reading my Bible more and more. Sometimes I would be up till the wee hours of the morning searching for a passage I had read once, so that I could answer one of their questions.

Diane and her family moved to another town, but her own questions persisted. She met with a local priest who answered none of them. "About this time, I was praying a lot for direction," she continues. "I didn't want to just write off these Jehovah's Witnesses as zealots. They had such faith!" Her drift back now begins to read like the stories of so many others of us. Diane met a woman in her parish, a former nun, who linked her up with several other women. They met once each week and read the Bible, prayed, socialized "and got some real answers to some real questions." The biggest revelation to Diane came shortly afterward. "Mostly I learned how much I don't know, while at the same time I have the same sense of faith that I have always had."

While these people found the Spirit in Protestant evangelical denominations, others were able to discover the Holy Spirit blowing fiercely in the Catholic Church's charismatic movement, which spread so enthusiastically and widely as part of Vatican II's fresh air.

Recall Bob. Raised as an Episcopalian who attended church regularly, he converted to Catholicism to marry. Bob reports that it took a Protestant to show him the charismatic way in a moment of crisis.

> For twenty years I "practiced" my Roman Catholic "faith." I went to Mass every Sunday out of a sense of obligation and a concern for not offending my wife. My faith, however, was not alive....
>
> When I was forty, things happened that made a profound spiritual impact on me. My work situation was extremely fragile. I was aware that what happened to me in this situation was primarily out of my control. I was suffering from the stress of the situation. A Pentecostal acquaintance came to my rescue. He told me about the Holy Spirit and gifts of the Holy Spirit. He even told me that my Catholic parish had a charismatic prayer group. I started going to this prayer group and my life changed. I received gifts of the Holy Spirit. I experienced God's presence in my life. I received a physical healing at a healing Mass....

The Catholic charismatic renewal doesn't appeal to everyone, of course. But some lost Catholics were attracted to the charismatic movement for many of the same reasons others "accepted Christ" in Protestant evangelical denominations: an emphasis on a personal relationship with a loving God, Bible study and emotion-filled worship services.

Called Home

Not every young adult looked outside the Catholic faith before finding it again. Some have simply dropped out of sight for a while without feeling the need to search elsewhere. Spiritual needs simply lay dormant for a time. But Catholic practices such as Mass, prayer and devotion to Mary and the saints were steady pulses reminding them of their ties to the Church. These were the home fires that were kept burning for members of our generation.

First, we'll look at Mass attendance. Almost every study taken over the last three decades points to declining Mass attendance among Catholics and especially among young adult Catholics. But hard numbers may be misleading since they don't track the ways in which people of any faith—or no faith at all—reach out to religious practices in the dark moments. How many of us, away from Mass for a long time, stop into a church on the way to catch a bus or driving home from work when our children are sick, our jobs are difficult or tenuous, or our parents are lying in hospital or nursing home beds? That's a number that can't be counted, but that doesn't mean that the faith being exhibited doesn't count.

Many began to stop going to Mass in high school when they no longer *had* to go with their parents. Mass attendance was thrown into the mixed bag of teenage rebellion against all things "parental." Many college students either didn't go at all or, more likely, went somewhere between frequently and only on Christmas, Easter, maybe Palm Sunday or Ash Wednesday. A woman in her forties remembers, "During college I went to Mass when I could. If I didn't go (most likely because of a hangover), I never felt as if I were sinning." Holy days of obligation went out the window, especially at a secular college or in the workplace, where the calendar was never marked in "Church time."

Although our generation missed Mass as much or more than previous generations, we didn't always feel bad about it. People report varying levels of guilt, misgivings or even a "So what? Who cares?" attitude. Maybe at the end of college, as "life" loomed, there was a tendency to duck into Mass or to make a visit to a church for a prayer or to light a candle again. Some people made commitments to go back at key moments in their lives—graduations, job changes, moves to new homes, deaths in the family.

The issue of Mass with kids can prevent people from returning to regular Mass attendance. With several children, it becomes increasingly harder to get all of them ready for Mass. Some young parents find it still harder because not every parish church has a "cry room." Parents don't want to disturb their neighbors in the pews at Mass. Some report nasty looks from older members of the congregation that seem to imply, with a disapproving sniff, "We didn't raise *our* kids that way." Some young parents split Mass. One week, one parent takes the kids while the other goes alone "to concentrate," as some say. The next week they switch. But often parents miss being together as a family at Mass. Even in a parish with a cry room, one mother says, "between viruses, teething and all that...we missed Mass a lot. But I still didn't feel guilty about it."

Francine, a thirty-three-year-old attorney, is married with three small children. She reports that her Mass attendance has ebbed and flowed with her little ones. She speaks for many members of our generation whose children got them thinking about their own faith. In Francine's case, it's her kids' squirming in the pews that has given her insight into her own ambivalence.

As a child, Francine attended weekly Mass reluctantly and then only sporadically during college and law school. "I always felt that God was with me, but the rigidity of attending Mass became too imposing," she writes.

However, my excuse not to attend Mass became my

children. [They are] beautiful, coy and rambunctious, [and] I feel their antics disturb those around me.... I had tried to raise the children to attend church as a routine, rather than as a chore. I believe I am failing. I now regularly attend church (or in a pinch alternate weeks with my husband) with my six-year-old daughter. Occasionally we bring the younger two (now ages two and three) but after a week or two, it usually proves to be too stressful and unsuccessful.

Focusing on my six-year-old, I see myself in her. I tried to explain the Mass to her and help her read along with the readings. Unfortunately, our lectors read from a different book...and the different words lose her. I am convinced that the basic Mass is just boring to a child. Until one begins to understand Catholic dogma, it is hard to follow—easy to turn from.

I remember sitting in church and wondering when would it end, when could I stop attending and basically, what was going on? Could it be that losing interest at a young age or just being a face in the crowd could lay the foundation for a later lapse in faith? I hope not. I consider myself lucky in that God always seems to welcome me, despite my lapses and despite others' stares. I only hope that my children know and understand that also....

My lapses were based in part upon boredom, lack of understanding, being healthy, young and invincible, and just being a nameless unconnected face in the crowd.

Prayer is the second traditional aspect of spirituality that calls large numbers of young adult Catholics back home to the Church. Prayer seems to be popular in general. *Newsweek* magazine, in a long article devoted to prayer in its March 31, 1997 issue, reported that over half of Americans questioned in a nationwide survey said they prayed every day while almost thirty percent said they prayed more than once each day. Prayers are even going high-tech: Jews can send a prayer via e-mail to Jerusalem where a company promises to run a hard copy of the prayer right over to the Western Wall and slip it into a crack, a customary way of asking God for help.

More specific statistics related to Catholics that were gathered in 1993 indicate that a little over half of our generation prays daily, although another thirty percent said they pray weekly or occasionally (*Laity: American and Catholic*, page 76). A more recent survey taken in late 1995 indicates that two-thirds of young adult Catholics (aged eighteen to thirty plus) surveyed say they pray alone frequently; another twenty-seven percent say they pray alone occasionally. In the latter survey, a further breakdown shows that in the older group (over thirty) eighty-one percent report praying frequently contrasted with fifty-two percent of eighteen- to twenty-two-year-olds (*Young Adult Research Report*, page 50).

When we return to prayer, it can feel like a long drink of water after days in the desert. Paulist Father Jac Campbell, who's been working to help young adult Catholics across the United States and Canada reconnect with the Church, says that he meets a lot of people our age who kept praying, or wanted to keep praying, even though they weren't otherwise active in the Church. "They have their grandfather's rosary," he says. "Just because they've been away doesn't mean they haven't been praying. They're not bad people. They've just been disengaged."

Many who have drifted back to Catholicism talk about prayer in terms very different from childhood prayers or a grandparent's rosary. Many adults are attracted by "felt" prayer that links us with our emotions, our affective sides, more than merely reciting prayers. Some people draw on meditative techniques from the Church's tradition as well as from other sources such as Eastern mysticism or yoga. In whatever ways we pray, we're glad to be doing so again.

Third, and perhaps surprisingly to some, our generation is rediscovering Mary, or maybe really discovering her for the first time. Though not the majority, a fair number of returning young adult Catholics included thanks and praise to Mary in the stories of their paths back to the Church. A generation that was generally raised without rosary beads and May crownings is looking to this strong woman from Nazareth as a model and guide with some frequency and enthusiasm. For others, Marian devotion is the one thing that stuck with them even as they drifted away from the Church.

Bob gives Mary all of the thanks for his return to the Church. After joining a charismatic prayer group through a Pentecostal friend, as we heard him recount earlier, Bob read a book written by a Lutheran about the people who say they've seen visions of Mary in Medjugorje. He remembers:

> I had a tremendous sense of truth: Mother Mary is real, Jesus is real, the Holy Spirit is true, the Roman Catholic Church is the true Church, Lourdes is true, Fatima is true, Guadalupe is true, Jesus will come again, our Heavenly Father loves us and gave his only Son so that we can have eternal life. For the first time in my life, I didn't just hope there was a God. I know there is....
>
> What brought...me back to spiritual reality? Mother Mary. I call her the best-kept secret of the post-Vatican II Roman Catholic Church. It took me twenty years of being a Roman Catholic to find what I needed in the Catholic Church. It took a Protestant to introduce me to the Holy Spirit and the charismatic renewal. It took another Protestant to introduce me to the role of Mother Mary in today's Church. It took Mother Mary to introduce me to her Son and enable me to see him on the cross through her eyes.

A woman from the Midwest asked that her name not be used because, as she put it, "This story belongs to our Blessed Mother. She can do with it whatever she wants. Give her the recognition." This woman sent a letter that she had written to a friend several years ago. She wanted to tell her friend about the grace that Mary has been to her. She never prayed a full rosary until 1992 and never understood essential beliefs about Mary and her role. But this woman now makes rosaries by hand for others. Why? She says that she wants to make up for lost time.

> You see, I long to serve the Blessed Virgin by spreading a devotion to her and her messages of prayer and conversion in any way she wants me to. I want to make up for the first thirty-six years of my life when I did not honor her or believe in her. In fact, I was quite disrespectful and angry at the Church for making a "Goddess" out of a very holy, but ordinary person, no matter how important her

role. She symbolized to me all that was wrong with the Catholic Church and my main feeling when she was mentioned was embarrassment....

May crowning was a fashion parade only. Ten years ago I remember kneeling alone in church and begging God to explain to me why Mary was so honored to be placed opposite Jesus? Wasn't he offended? How did she fit in? It just didn't make sense to me.

She considered joining a Protestant evangelical group, but after deep prayer and a strong sense of the presence of Mary, she reports that she is back home in the Catholic Church thanks to the Blessed Mother: "It is only through her help I have for the first time in my life become truly and joyfully Catholic."

Whose Church Is It, Anyway?

Drifting back to the Church—finally becoming "joyfully Catholic"—takes pilgrims along many paths, as we've seen. As difficult as the task of returning is, it seems even tougher once we arrive "back home" because of an increasingly bitter fight going on within the Catholic Church as to what Catholicism is and means to us today. All of this confusion leaves our generation asking, "Whose Church is it, anyway?"

The two wings of the Church are often far more vocal and visible than the more moderate group in the middle. When Pope John Paul II visited Denver in 1993, talk shows and news programs were filled with so-called liberal and conservative Catholics, each group trying to promote its view of the Church and to paint the other side as the lunatic fringe. "Liberals" tried to present every "conservative" as an abortion protester who doesn't mind seeing doctors and nurses shot; "conservatives" charged "liberal dissenters" with being "smorgasbord Catholics" or dismissed them as not *really* Catholic.

This is a great and dangerous divide. We have become a Church of "us" and "them." Given this situation, it seems logical to ask why anti-Catholics waste their time fighting us. We're dividing our own house just fine. In many cases, each side argues that theirs is the "real" or "true" Church that has kept the faith since the Second Vatican Council. Catholics frequently argue about Vatican II: The Church hasn't gone far enough in implementing Vatican II, says one side, while the other side wonders if Catholics went too far in the Council's initial aftermath. The fight can get ugly. When the "right" accuses the "left" of not being Catholic, the "left" accuses the "right" of being self-righteous and accusatory, of locking the Catholic faith in time through rigid practices and closed minds.

Teri wrote in a cover letter accompanying her story:

> Truly there is a split in the American and the Roman Catholic Church. Those other young "conservatives" such as myself realize this as well. I pray that your book will illustrate what we traditionalists have known all along. We were lost because we were victim to the radicals of the 1960's, 1970's and even current tenured faculty at our "esteemed" Catholic universities. The time has come, and finally the pendulum is swinging back. We were "right" all along.

Teri's last phrase, "We were 'right' all along," has become something of a rallying cry for those members of our generation who have embraced a more traditional Catholicism. It is interesting to note that some who express this sentiment were born after the Council's changes and never actually experienced the "brand" of Catholicism to which they are now returning.

Martin, who is a little older than Teri, writes from Pennsylvania with much of the same tone and passion. But Martin argues from another perspective. Although he is quite taken with the writings of C. S. Lewis, who is frequently read by the "right" as well as the "left," he is starting to reject other authors favored by the "right":

> For awhile I was taken with the "apologetics" of Scott Hahn, Karl Keating and Peter Kreeft, and their work made an impression on me. At this point, however, I consider these men a bit too much on the triumphalist, right-wing, "apologetics-making" side of the Church....I guess it's obvious, huh? There are "sides." I have a theory that the "Council of Trent" Church is at war with the "Vatican II Church," and it's in the hands of God where we're going.

Is our generation in some way especially vulnerable to a split into factions? It may be that people favor one side or another because they are looking for certainty or absolute answers after so much questioning and seeking. Several experienced young adult ministers see the reach for "the" answer from the "right" or the "left" as a desperate cry for security, even though it leads to a kind of fundamentalism.

According to John Roberto, a leader of the *Young Adult Research Report*, the call of opposite sides is alluring because people feel groundless. He thinks this is especially true of those who gravitate to the "right":

> It's security, structure, certainty in a world that's just the opposite. Religion is an oasis for them. They cling to an image of the Church which answers this profound human need that they have. It's a Church that just doesn't exist anymore. They have no memory of it. It's an idealized vision. It's the clarity of a black-and-white world that they hunger for.

Another experienced young adult minister agrees. Jesuit Father Joseph Burke, who links spirituality and psychology in his work, says:

> People are looking to have a mature adult faith just as we try to develop a mature personality. To have a mature faith means no longer the faith of a child, which is totally accepting because others say it. And it's not adolescence either, which is pure questioning. As they move toward a mature young adult faith, they can live what they believe with a sense of personal honesty and integrity. That's hard.

Sharon Parks offers a sociologist's explanation of why young adult Catholics are being pulled by two sides, each of which promises the "real" truth of Catholicism. It's worth quoting her to make this delicate, easily misunderstood point which is too often colored by politics. Although Parks is speaking generally about the ways young adults are captured by cults—and this is certainly not a statement or even a hint that "right" and "left" Catholics are cultists—her point is important for our generation of Catholics. The key, she says, is our vulnerability.

This vulnerability is only sharpened when young adults can find no effective connection with society. They are, therefore, particularly vulnerable if there is no network of belonging that can incarnate a significant sense of connection against the threat of meaninglessness. Young adults require a meaningful ideology (a dream) and a grounding community (*The Critical Years*, page 99).

Our context is frequently the groundless, disconnected Catholic experience of our childhood. This fact causes us to search for a grounded, Catholic meaning and a network of like-minded Catholics. But because our education was poor, returning members of our generation don't necessarily have the background to sift through what we hear. And sometimes we don't want to because if we think we've found a grounding community, we are reluctant to question its beliefs and attitudes. The ideological extremes of the "right" or "left" wings of the Church often seem to offer the correct, unquestionable answers and foundations we crave.

This is not to say that all returning Catholics split into factions. Older members of our generation have both positive and negative reactions to what they experienced before the Council. Some are nostalgic for the old ways, others felt liberated by the changes. Younger members of the same group take the post-Vatican II perspective for granted because they never knew anything else and yet still feel attracted to the mystery and transcendence of the Church they never knew.

The "right" and "left" are not our only choices. Teri talks about the pendulum swinging back to the right; Martin sees a war between two Churches. The pendulum image can be interpreted another way. Did the Church swing to the far left immediately after Vatican II in the 1960's and 1970's, and then to the far right in the 1980's and 1990's? Can we find a middle ground? We may be guilty of spending so much time talking—and arguing and accusing—about Catholic matters that we have forgotten to be Christian. "It's my Church: love it or leave it," is a wholly unchristian sentiment. The battle lines have been drawn, but what happened to the shared journey of faith?

A number of Catholics in our generation try hard to avoid

the right-left split. Many young adult Catholics have decided that before we change anyone else's mind we should, as Voltaire pointed out in another context, cultivate our own gardens first. We see our shared spiritual journey as far too crucial to waste our time in what we see as destructive politics. Some of us, instead, look at the trees of our lives instead of trying to replant the forest. According to this perspective, our infighting and defensiveness can cause us to forget that God is in the details. The struggle to be a good Catholic takes place in the dozens of decisions we make or affirm each day, not just in major policy battles fought out in state capitals or school board meetings, important though they are. We can help bring the Kingdom closer each day, not just by swinging the votes of senators, but also by making sure the little old lady next door doesn't feel lonely tonight.

Married With Children

The topics we've covered so far represent major subjects for the Church in bringing our generation back. The spirit of Protestant evangelicals and Catholic charismatics; the comfort of Mass, prayer and devotion to Mary; and even the security offered by different, though often opposing groups within the Church, all serve in their own ways to draw diverse people back into the Church. But for our generation, as for any generation of Catholics, the biggest factor in returning to the practice of the faith is getting married and having children.

Getting married and having kids make us think seriously about our Catholic faith again. Research shows that this is a natural "rebound." New parents will often turn back to the Church for advice and direction in raising their children in the faith even if they've been disconnected from Catholicism for some time.

Roof found the experience of family life and raising kids at the top of the list of reasons why people return to their childhood faiths, even with long gaps of nonparticipation. The birth of a child prompts parents to think about the meaning of their lives and their children's lives in new, personal and deep ways. New parents tap into a larger faith community for guidance and a sense of belonging to others who are experiencing the same emotions and challenges of parenthood from a religious point of view (*A Generation of Seekers*, pages 156-161).

Roof also noted that adult children who had close relationships with their own parents, even within a fairly rigid upbringing, were less likely to drift away from their faith and more likely to return if they did take a break. Some of those who sent in their stories for this book had been given the magazine clipping by their parents. In other cases, the parents themselves mailed in accounts of their children's stories.

Prompted by a letter from her mother, Elizabeth tells her story of returning to the Catholic Church because of her own responsibilities as a mother, even though she's had a rocky path home. She now lives in South Carolina. Elizabeth recounts that she was "brought up in the 'old' ways. Some of those ways I still practice to this day." Her family began to lose sight of the Church, however. Although Elizabeth and her older brother received Confirmation, the sacraments stopped at Communion for their younger brothers. Her parents divorced. In high school, Elizabeth hooked up with a group of Christian schoolmates and received a Bible.

> I still have this book today and relate to it constantly. As I look back to this Bible of my youth, I have passages highlighted or underlined. It reminds me of my comfort in God through troubled times. I remember I would attend Mass very seldom. I guess I lost interest.

When Elizabeth joined the military after high school around 1976, she went to Mass just to get away from her barracks. She married a Methodist man. The Catholic Church continued to call her, although she never felt fully comfortable there because of her unsettling experiences of two Churches.

> As my age progressed I felt I needed God and the Church in my life more and more. As I proceeded to go to Mass, I really felt a little out of place because things had changed so much. As I got married (received another sacrament)

and became a parent myself, I found I needed the stability of the Church more and more.... Because of my marriage to a Methodist, I knew the religious upbringing of my daughter was solely mine. This also brought me back closer to the Church, but by now things had changed so much from when I was a child I really felt lost.

After two years of military service in Germany, Elizabeth returned to the United States with her baby, who had been baptized Catholic. She and her husband divorced.

Shortly after...I started going back to Church. Again I felt a little out of place. However, the priest at the Church I attended somehow grabbed my attention and I began going to Church on a more regular basis. In addition, my daughter started attending catechism. I knew also that I had to set an example. My daughter and I continued to go to Church.

Other members of our generation are also being sobered by the experience of raising children. Realizing that their religious education had often been poor and left them with feelings of emptiness, they don't want to see yet another generation go through the same thing. Raising kids gives them a sense of their duties as Catholic parents *and* of their responsibilities to care for their own religious lives, too.

Cheryl has already related her feelings that as a child the Church made her feel guilty instead of making her feel loved, as she experiences the Church today. After marrying a man who had little interest in religion, Cheryl's attention to her own religious practices began to flag, as well. In the 1980's, they raised their children as nominal Catholics, just going through the motions. Her kids, she says now, were "Catholic only by virtue of their Baptism. My children [went] to CCD classes so they could receive the proper sacraments at the right age."

But Cheryl was brought up short. She realized that she was only perpetuating the religious problems she had as a child. Cheryl was setting the stage for her children to duplicate the mistakes she'd made. "My support of their faith [and] lessons of God's love [were] repeating in some aspects what I had received: no Spirit, no Life, no Love, really no God."

Then, a few years ago when she was in her forties, Cheryl heard a Franciscan Capuchin priest talk about the love and goodness of God during a meeting of school mothers. Bearing out the statistics and findings of research studies, Cheryl connected with a network of other young parents going through similar faith journeys. The parents' journeys were sparked by their children's Catholic experiences. As we've seen often, her drift back to a real relationship with the Church started with a personal invitation and was followed up in a good experience with an active parish and a lively liturgy.

> It was as if this was the time. Friends had changed parishes and were enthusiastic about their new parish. They talked about young families, warmth, high attendance and participation at 10 a.m. Mass with a positive, young (forty-ish) priest. "Come, join us. The priest is so up, you feel good after Mass." That was the invitation. And that priest, unknown to me, was the same Capuchin who first really made me hear, "God is Good. God is Love."

Like Elizabeth and Cheryl, Jim is concerned that the next generation of young Catholics, those born in the 1980's and 1990's, doesn't fall away, too. Jim's faith had been energized in college through a nondenominational Christian fellowship. He reports that he and his wife, whom he met through a parish choir, have deepened their faith and marriage through praying and reading the Bible together. Now stronger in their faith, they are working on passing it to their own kids.

> We recently had our fourth child and we think the most important thing we can teach them is to make God number one in their lives. We pray often with our children—before meals, before bed, and we teach them to pray when they are having difficulties or are joyous. We read from the Bible to our children and we talk to them often about God.... Our prayer is that our children will know God and walk with him throughout their lives. We don't want our children to be among those who fall away from the Church and need to find their way back!

Some Catholics fear it may be too late for the generations to follow. Ann, a woman in her late fifties, now realizes that in fact she *didn't* hand on the faith to her daughter, a member of our generation of young adult Catholics. Ann's parents and grandparents held their faith very strongly and took it very seriously. They gave her a good Catholic education in the 1940's and 1950's, but at age sixteen she left the Church and school to marry in a civil ceremony. She had a baby girl but divorced after five years of marriage. Ann then spent more than thirty years away from the practice of Catholicism. She's back—"all the way home, at peace with Jesus, Mary, and Joseph"—as she writes. But, she adds,

> The sad part of my story is my daughter and my grandchildren. During the period of time that I was neglecting my spiritual life, my daughter was being deprived of that beautiful foundation I had enjoyed as a child. Although she was baptized and received Holy Communion, attended Mass, etc., she didn't get the benefit of the living example of family. She grew up through the changes of Vatican II that occurred while I was "out to lunch." I sent her off to Church with anyone who happened to be going, paying no attention to the need for parental guidance. Today she is married out of the Catholic Church, has two beautiful children who are baptized out of the faith.... My cross today is in knowing that her alienation from the Church is all a result of my indifference.
>
> I think that many of this lost generation...probably have had a similar experience. These children [are] all lacking in proper education as a result of the complacency and indifference of parents like me. I can only pray that Jesus, Mary and Joseph will help me to lead her now to where I should have been taking her all these lost years.

There are more optimistic stories. Neil and Pat from Michigan report that their thirteen-year-old granddaughter, Casey, is leading her father (that's Neil and Pat's son, from our generation), back to the Catholic Church. Over the years, whenever they visited their son and his family in Kentucky, Neil and Pat would take Casey to Mass on Sunday.

Casey was impressed and met friends of hers from school. When she was twelve, she expressed interest in taking instruction in the Catholic faith. We, of course, encouraged her, as did her parents. With the help of her mother and father and friends, she attended CCD classes and was privately instructed by teachers in the RCIA program. Her mother, who is not Catholic, attended the RCIA program so she could better understand what Casey was studying. One year later on Holy Saturday 1997, Casey [joined] the Catholic Church, was baptized, confirmed and received her first Holy Communion. We, her grandparents, were very honored to be her godparents.

Her mother wants to become a Catholic, also. She must, however, file for an annulment, as she was previously married. Our son would come back to the Church and be married by a priest. He will do this and hopefully they will all be Catholic once again.

Casey's faith has made us all aware of the power of prayer.

There are, it seems, happy endings after all.

PART THREE

Settling Back Home

So far, we've spent time listening to the voices of our friends and neighbors in the generation formed in the wake of Vatican II. Whether we have drifted away from the Church and are, at least to some degree, drifting back, or whether we've stayed in the Church all along and are looking for a way to be more active in our expression of Catholicism, now it's time to consider how we might best settle in.

This part builds on the previous two. We've heard our stories and explored how they fit into standard patterns of spiritual and psychological development. Having done that, it's now time to look for some good hints for easing our way to feeling comfortable again—or perhaps comfortable for the first time—as sons and daughters in the Catholic Church. Let's discuss ways to address our particular needs and desires with what we've learned so far about our pilgrims' paths, spiritual surfing, shopping around through the stormy seas of Vatican II and its new "brand" of Catholicism, and our stumbling through difficult social and political times. As we've done all along, we'll let the people at ground zero speak for themselves. In this case, we'll turn our ears to several experienced young adult ministers who have met with, spoken to, helped, and especially *heard* us over the last two decades.

What We Want

We've indicated that we want a spiritual, not an institutional experience of the Catholic faith. We want a personal relationship with our faith and spirituality. For some this may be affective and emotion-filled; for others it may be intellectually challenging. We want an "owned" faith, one that we've chosen as adults, not a faith that is imposed on us. We're making a decision as adults to live our lives as baptized, confirmed, committed Catholics. We want a faith that helps us connect Sunday with Monday through Friday, a genuine faith strongly connected to our way of life.

The *Young Adult Research Report* compiled the top ten responses to the question, "What are young adults looking for in a Church today?" asked in a national survey in 1995. This top ten list summarizes what we've been crying out for and what our parishes must provide in their response to our need for "connectedness" and identity. We want to share our gifts, our experiences in the world and our enthusiasm. But we can only participate if we experience the following in the Church:

1. a sense of belonging and community; opportunities for involvement in Church life;

2. dynamic liturgies;

3. spiritual growth and enrichment;

4. religious education;

5. guidance and direction;

6. acceptance and support;

7. opportunities for service; a chance to make a difference;

8. social activities;

9. a community of common values;

10. inspiration and rejuvenation.
   (*Young Adult Research Report*, page 34)

Beyond these ten, however, we want to connect specifically with our Catholic heritage and forge a Catholic identity, but we want it to be a transformed Catholic identity for our times. We're looking for an experience of Catholicism that gives us both the spirituality we crave and the education we need. We want to be recognized for our unique place in the Church. We want people to listen to our own concerns instead of assuming that our issues are no different than those of the generations that have gone before us.

We want the Church to recognize that we're on the road to discovery about ourselves and our faith, but we're not quite there yet. While some latch onto a wing of Catholicism that says, "We've got the answers," others believe it's not that easy or clear-cut when it comes to feeling spiritually at home in a place we haven't visited in a while, sometimes a long while.

As Kevin from Canada puts it, we want to find a home but we also need time and space. He offers this advice to those who might be waiting to welcome adults returning to the Catholic Church.

> To you who have always felt at home, try to remember that what you see in us is not lack of commitment but a lack of confidence. We've been on our own for so long that the warmth of your welcome makes even the shortest return visit all the more awkward. I often feel we don't deserve such a greeting. I, like many of the "lost generation" of pre- and post-Vatican II Catholics, am still returning. I am still on my way. Not "back" but rather "alongside of" a Church still in transition. An individual and an institution both in the process of becoming.

Our bishops recognized in *Sons and Daughters of the Light* that we're on this kind of a spiritual search for religious meaning and identity. But how do we find it, especially in a parish commmunity that may have been set up according to much different models than the home we seek?

Many of those who want to return to the Catholic Church feel tentative or scared. Paulist Father Jac Campbell, who has been working with young adults since the 1980's, says that many of them don't feel worthy of returning, don't know how to come back to the Church or are surprised at the Church they find.

> They bring a fear that they're not holy enough or smart enough that they can come back in.... Years ago, if we drifted away we'd just go to Confession and come back to the same parish. Today we're finding people who have

moved geographically. When they return they find a social order that's different.

Perhaps our most basic desire is this: We want to be heard, and then we want to connect to our faith in a way that speaks to us in our language. We want people to reach out to where we are spiritually and physically. Young adult ministers in the diocese of Buffalo, for example, reached out to disconnected Catholics of our generation across western New York state, beginning in the bars and places where young people gathered. Their information sessions quickly drew almost a thousand young adults, and they put together a successful program called QUEST to follow up on the interest and enthusiasm they found.

Reaching out is key. Jesuit Father Joseph Burke started the young adult ministry in the Archdiocese of New York and has been working in that ministry for more than a decade. In his experience, young adults drift away from the Church when they don't feel connected or even noticed. "I hear that people left the Catholic Church for awhile not because of dogmatic problems. I never hear that someone left because they didn't believe in transubstantiation," Father Burke says. "There was some personal affront, an insult. They felt ignored, not listened to."

The answer, according to Father Burke, is the idea of "connectedness." "It comes down to people looking to connect with relationships. People want to connect with relationships with themselves, with God, with the Church, with someone special." The annual New York archdiocesan gatherings for young adults are now called "Connecting Conferences."

Landings, a Paulist program designed to help young adult Catholics reconnect with their Catholicism, began in Seattle in the 1980's. Landings has operated in more than two dozen dioceses in Alaska, Oregon, Louisiana, Ohio, Massachusetts and elsewhere, including several Canadian cities. More than sixty thousand people have attended these sessions.

The program organizers, led by Father Campbell, realized that our generation wants to be listened to and then reconnected with the Church. "There seems to be some need to want to talk, to say, 'This is what happened to me. This is how I got hurt. This is why I want to come back.'" In a series of informal meetings in people's homes, young adults tell their stories. There's no judgment or scolding. People talk about their experiences, not their catechisms, although the conversations often turn to next steps. Some end up celebrating the Sacrament of Reconciliation, going over the creed, learning about the sacraments or pursuing particular questions. Many simply begin to repair relationships and emotions that have blocked the return home to the Catholic Church for years.

Landings organizers say that this personal approach, especially the shared stories, binds people together and encourages the idea that our journeys are personal but not necessarily strange, shameful or even entirely unique. After listening to thousands of stories at Landings sessions, Father Campbell has this observation:

> It's the dynamic of being listened to. They feel heard and known and wanted. It's the very idea that people are interested in hearing your religious lives, your parents and grandparents' religious lives, your ups and downs.
>
> They're back for a sense of belonging to a religious family. There's a little bit of "How do we do this? How do we do that?" Most want to get back to the sacraments. Many of our people have tried all kinds of religious adventures. Now they just want to come back and put it together. Now they're going to take another look at Catholicism. It's best if they're met by people instead of doctrine. They know enough of the answers. They have to reconnect to the sacramental life of the Catholic Church.
>
> Programs that call for estranged and angry Catholics pull estranged and angry people. The other group really wants to get back. They're not angry. They've done a lot of healing. They're ready to make peace.

For the most part, our generation of Catholics doesn't carry the same anger that the generation immediately preceding us often does. Especially those who are younger are more confused than angry. Our experience of the Church was not necessarily that of an oppressive, controlling institution. More likely, as we've heard from some of the voices in this book, it was a sense that nothing was solid, nothing was absolute. For many of us, it wasn't a question of needing to question or even break the rules; rather, it often seemed as though the rules never existed in the first place.

Once we decide we're ready to reconnect, then, we're often most enthused about a newly rediscovered spirituality and how it may or may not fit in with our Catholic heritage. In Manhattan, for example, a two-day workshop with the provocative title "The New Mysticism" drew almost 1,100 people, most of them young adults, who learned about the history, tradition and practice of mystical prayer in the Catholic Church. People were amazed to find that what they were searching for in the New Age was actually waiting for them at home in Catholicism, and in a way that offered roots as well as wings.

Father Burke was there. He notes that it was as if the participants found a new elixir of life. This spirit of excitement was especially hopeful since many of the participants had long been searching and trying out lesser versions of the rich Catholic prayer and spiritual heritage. The people at that mysticism workshop were like some in the Landings program who experienced different religious adventures but wanted to put it all together within their Catholic upbringing. Father Burke thinks that this kind of spiritual enthusiasm, combined with a grounding education, may just be the right mix to attract and keep those in our generation who are trying to reconnect with the Catholic Church:

> All of us need some grounding for meaning for our lives.
> All those alternatives just simply didn't fit the bill. So
> there's a renewed thirst for spiritual meaning that became
> very much alive in people. Young adults are not
> necessarily looking for spiritual meaning from an
> institution. They're looking for personal meaning and
> trying to see if the Church can offer them a sense of
> rootedness.
>
> The Church must recognize this fact, the phenomena *du
> jour*. The Church must attempt to develop a rich resource it
> already has, namely the spirituality of the Catholic faith.

Instead of emphasizing rules, regulations and rituals (but don't throw them out), just shift the outreach programs that will address individual and communal spirituality.

Within people, there is a need for that connection with the transcendent. It's almost as if mentally or psychologically we're wired to a transcendent power. In order to find meaning, we have to address that need.

John Roberto agrees. He says that the Church needs to connect with people by going where they are emotionally and spiritually. That's a better approach, in his eyes, than pulling them to a place where they don't want to be, at least not yet. His advice is to tap into their spiritual yearning and connect their faith into their work weeks, struggles and roles as Catholics, spouses or parents. The challenge is to make Catholicism relevant to people's lives and to understand that the two go together.

Simply put, we want help finding a way to connect our Catholicism to today's society, to values for living and to our spirituality, prayer and faith journeys. We want to return to the Church, but we want someone there to greet us. We don't want to feel that we're the only ones who care about the fact that we *want* to reconnect with the Catholic faith as it's being lived and worked out in the spirit of Vatican II.

Forging a New Catholic Identity in the Spirit of Vatican II

Vatican II was the key event in our religious lives and Catholic identity. Vatican II fundamentally changed the way all Catholics see, feel and experience Catholicism. As Father Burke observes from his twin perspective as a spiritual director and a clinical psychologist:

Initially, one of the things that Vatican II offered was a paradigmatic shift in people's minds. That shift encompassed a change from [people] valuing their faith and having a sense of self-acceptance from the Church as an *external* validator to an *internal* validator. Vatican II opened up a shift in culture. It opened up all kinds of possibilities. Then, people saw that there were a lot of excesses in terms of only internal validation.... And now we're swinging back into external validation. That's why people want approval. It's going to have to come back to some middle ground.

Clearly, for our generation the middle ground between internal and external validation will not define what it means to be Catholic in the same way our parents' generations did. Our parents were raised to give the *Baltimore Catechism*'s answers. And they lived in a Catholic culture that clearly reinforced their religious identity for them. There were definite markers that said, "Catholics do this. Catholics don't do that." While many of those identity markers still exist, they are not as embedded in our everyday culture. That's a crucial difference, and part of the reason our generation lost its bearings. At the same time, the idea that we all know internally what it means to be Catholic and can determine this for ourselves as individuals runs the risk of destroying any communal sense of our identity as a Church. So, we're still asking, "What makes me Catholic?"

Sometimes I envy Catholics of my parents' generation. When our mothers were in school, they knew they had to wear a little veil to Mass. My dad feared the wrath of his brother Benny, the formidable head of the family, when according to family legend their youngest sibling Louie ate a nickel piece of candy the morning of his First Communion and so couldn't receive. It was a big issue for the whole family and my Uncle Benny took care of business with Uncle Louie! There were celebrations of Forty Hour devotions, novenas and Stations of the Cross that helped guide them. Parishes sponsored organizations for boys, girls, men and women, and people knew that they were expected to belong to these groups. This offered both ongoing formation and also a social outlet.

Decades ago, movies raised some of these Catholic markers to an accepted cultural standard, sometimes in subtle ways. Amanda Wingfield, the mother in Tennessee Williams' *The Glass Menagerie*, frets that she'll have to make a salmon loaf because a Catholic guest is coming to dinner on Friday night. Bing Crosby sang "Tooralooraloora" as he went his way. Pat O'Brien kept gangsters praying as they walked to a final penance in the electric chair or gas chamber. Playing Father Flanagan, Spencer Tracy tamed Mickey Rooney to establish Boys Town—and won an Oscar in the process.

Today, I hear many of our parents' generation—and, curiously, even some of our own—lamenting the loss of these customs as they reflect on the "good old days." I've had enough experience of looking back to know that the good old days were never really as perfect as we may imagine. Years build up a gauzy aura that disproportionately highlights the positive and filters the pain. All of those rituals were indeed spiritual aids and guides: actions or objects people could grab onto for support, security and identity. They pointed Catholics in the right direction. We need rosary beads, statues and candles to do that sometimes.

But was that age as golden as our parents think? Could they have been so busy doing things that they didn't know *why* they were kneeling at the Corpus Christi procession or crowning Mary? And how is it possible that people in their twenties and thirties pine for those days of Latin Masses when they never experienced them growing up? Is it nostalgia? Revisionist history? An attempt to recreate a past that never existed in the first place?

Let me suggest an explanation that arises from the voices of our generation. Many of us are crying out for a Catholic identity that's internally meaningful to us. In the absence of deep learning, some spiritual directors and psychologists observe, people sometimes grab onto external rituals as an entry point. But it's important not to substitute the outer ritual itself for the meaning it's meant to reflect within. Those rituals of our parents' generation served a good purpose. But what happened when they became so rote that they failed to go beneath the surface? In our own century, when not eating meat on Friday became a routine, did Catholics forget that abstinence was meant as a reminder that Jesus died on a cross for us on a Friday? Did they miss the irony of forgoing meat for an exotic seafood dinner? Without an awareness of the underlying meaning, the ritual became empty and part of the mustiness that John XXIII was trying to clear out when he opened the

Church's windows to let in Vatican II's fresh air.

Pining for the old days, then, can easily translate into a desire for a form that had lost its content. Perhaps some in the Church had lost sight of the fact that who we are is more important than what we do, though of course the two are related. The core of what makes us Catholic may have been lost in practices that had become devoid of real devotion. On the other hand, in the post-Vatican II zeal to revamp the externals, the reformers may have also thrown out the underlying significance, what some people refer to as "throwing out the baby with the bath water." Assuming that people were relying on some of these practices as crutches, the reformers may have discarded some handy and useful aids to defining Catholic identity.

Part of the loss of identity has also been the loss of a sense of awe, mystery and wonder that some remember from pre-Vatican II childhoods. This was the case in several stories we have heard here. Reaffirming a sense of awe and majesty might reinstill in us both respect for each other and a sense of reverence for the holy that is the nucleus of our loving, internal relationship with God. Our old rituals once stood for something. But if we simply bring them back for the sake of nostalgia or, more ominously, in the mistaken notion that by resurrecting deeds we will somehow magically bring back "faith," as several young adult Catholic students have forcefully told me in my courses, are we running the risk of repeating past patterns of barren action?

The answer to what it means to be Catholic is far more complex than the old *Baltimore Catechism* once let on. Coming to an understanding of our faith and what being Catholic means for us has been difficult. We don't always understand or even know our Catholic heritage because many of us had a poor religious education. We have seen some of our generation searching in other religious experiences—mostly the New Age and Protestant evangelical denominations—for a tradition of mystical and affective prayer that is actually rooted firmly in our Catholic tradition.

Finding a balance is never easy. How can we accept others'

well-meant efforts, learn from their (and our own) mistakes and successes, and do something about our unique situation? Some members of our generation seem eager to bring our diverse experiences to bear on moving forward. Jean Marie was battered by some tough times that represent most of the events we've been exploring.

> I have felt ignored by the Church hierarchy (it was especially offensive to me to have priests not look me in the eyes when we talk); belittled by the culture for being "religious"; discouraged by my siblings' "falling away"; ridiculed [and] antagonized by non-Catholic Christians; disappointed by older Catholics fighting over "the changes" in the Church...; frustrated by inadequate answers to my questions about morals and Church teaching; and despairing [because of] the hypocrisy of all of us who call ourselves "Christians."

Still, she and her husband sound ready to get to work.

> Through the Lord's faithfulness and my perseverance, I'm an active member of the Church now.... We recently returned from a week-long retreat in Arkansas and have heard the Lord's call to a more radical way of following him. We're not sure where he'll take us, but we are committed—heart, mind, body, soul and spirit—to follow him wherever he takes us. We are growing in holiness together, which was one of our marriage vows, and hope to be a light for others.

In fact, having experienced so much turmoil within our Church, our society and ourselves, our generation may be the right one to find the successful middle way. For instance, if we decide to refrain from meat on Fridays in a new, thoughtful, faith-inspired attempt to go beyond the pre-Vatican rote practice to the original reason for the ritual, maybe we will be getting somewhere. It will be a small step, no doubt, but a meaningful move forward nonetheless. Likewise, restoring awe in the sacramental presence and getting rid of our embarrassment at unintellectual emotion may be a way to face our inability or unwillingness to celebrate the wonderful mystery of God. By reestablishing a solid intellectual, emotional and psychological grounding for the practice of our faith, we can proudly identify ourselves as Catholics in our secular, professional contacts without making apologies.

There's No Place Like Home

Our journey, as we've heard, has been particularly characterized by our searching, questioning and even challenging Catholicism. This is not necessarily a bad thing or something to be ashamed of, especially when sharing our stories with one another or when talking with a spiritual director. It's important to remember that questioning often leads to a deeper, more solid faith. In many ways, there's nothing new in our search. We've wandered, yes, but so did Saint Francis, a playboy as a young adult but a faithful, innovative Catholic who was on the cutting edge of his society once he decided to accept his faith as a mature man. What Saint Francis found, and what many in our generation have shared, is that when we come back to the Church, we find that it offered what we wanted all along. In the Middle Ages, the scholastic theologian Peter Abelard declared that by doubting religious issues, we begin to inquire about them. Through that inquiry, we will eventually come to the truth. This method was endorsed, Abelard said, by God who told us to seek so that we may find.

Wade Clark Roof offers an update of this medieval method. Thinking about the evidence gathered by the survey of Baby Boomers and their spiritual journeys, Roof concluded that the young adult experience of a plurality of religious choices might actually result in *stronger* institutional affiliations with a religious group.

> Americans will increasingly make religious and spiritual choices on the basis of their preferences, which will help to emancipate faith from ascriptive loyalties. Personal autonomy rather than family heritage or religious background will increasingly be the basis on which one relates to the sacred. What a person chooses rather than is

born into will be decisive. (*A Generation of Seekers*, page 259)

Viewed through the prism of both medieval theology and twentieth-century sociology, then, our generation might just be poised to be the strongest leaders for the third millennium of Christianity. We've surfed through spiritual choices to select Catholicism as our own. We rode the stormy waves of Vatican II. Because of our experiences of drifting, reaching out and settling back home, maybe we have the best chance to find that precious middle ground. We can take the best but avoid the worst from the "right" and "left" wings that threaten to divide Catholicism and allow many Catholics to fall into the wide chasm that threatens to separate what should be the seamless garment of the Church.

Finally, we must remember that the Church is still in process, just like all of us are on our own spiritual journeys. In a special way, however, each individual member of our generation has been intimately and uniquely linked with the Church's journey over the last three decades. The implementation of Vatican II has been evolving since the 1960's and our personal religious journeys have been closely tied to the Church's "ups" and "downs." In essence, we've been living through the creative tensions of Vatican II. We're still witnessing the battle for the legacy of Vatican II. It's been taking place in our lives, in our parishes, in our Church. We must help the Church find a middle way between the rigidity of the *Baltimore Catechism* and the "Jesus-is-a-warm-fuzzy" school. The Catholic faith planted in us by our parents and teachers may have lain dormant for many years, but it is still there waiting to grow and bear fruit when we are ready. We will come home, only to discover that all along we had within the Church and within the Catholic faith in our hearts what we longed for and looked for in so many other places.

For Further Reading

Books

Alberigo, Giuseppe, et al., eds. *The Reception of Vatican II.* Washington, D.C.: The Catholic University of America Press, 1987.

Butler, Francis J., ed. *American Catholic Identity: Essays in an Age of Change.* Kansas City, Mo.: Sheed & Ward, 1994.

Davidson, James D., et al. *The Search for Common Ground: What Unites and Divides Catholic Americans.* Huntington, Ind.: Our Sunday Visitor, 1997.

D'Antonio, William V., et al. *Laity, American and Catholic: Transforming the Church.* Kansas City, Mo.: Sheed & Ward, 1996.

Dulles, Avery, S.J. *The Reshaping of Catholicism.* San Francisco: Harper & Row, 1988.

Duquin, Lorene Hanley. *Could You Ever Come Back to the Catholic Church?* Staten Island, N.Y.: Alba House, 1997.

Fagin, Gerald M., ed. *Vatican II: Open Questions and New Horizons.* Wilmington, Del.: Michael Glazier, 1984.

Fowler, James. *Becoming Adult, Becoming Christian: Adult Development and Christian Faith.* San Francisco: Harper & Row, 1984.

Kennedy, Eugene. *Tomorrow's Catholics, Yesterday's Church.* New York: Harper & Row, 1988.

Latourelle, Rene, ed. *Vatican II: Assessment and Perspectives. Twenty-Five Years After (1962-1987)*. 3 vols. New York: Paulist Press, 1988-1989.

Ludwig, Robert A. *Reconstructing Catholicism for a New Generation*. New York: Crossroad, 1995.

National Conference of Catholic Bishops. *Sons and Daughters of the Light: A Pastoral Plan for Ministry with Young Adults*. United States Catholic Conference Publishing Services, 1997.

Parks, Sharon. *The Critical Years: The Young Adult Search for a Faith to Live By*. San Francisco: Harper & Row, 1986.

Roof, Wade Clark. *A Generation of Seekers: The Spiritual Journeys of the Baby Boom Generation*. San Francisco: HarperSanFrancisco, 1993.

Williams, Andrea S., and James D. Davidson. "Catholic Conceptions of Faith: A Generational Analysis." *Sociology of Religion* 57:3 (1996), pp. 273-289.

Organizations

Center for Ministry Development
John Roberto, Director
P.O. Box 699
Naugatuck, CT 06770
203-723-1622 phone

Landings. Welcoming Returning Catholics: A Paulist Ministry
Fr. Jac Campbell, C.S.P., National Director
5 Park St.
Boston, MA 02108
e-mail: jacsp@aol.com
617-720-5986 phone
617-723-2170 fax

Joan A. Horn, National Coordinator
3311 Big Bend
Austin, TX 78731
e-mail: horn@mail.utexas.edu
512-452-7566 phone

National Catholic Young Adult Ministry Association
7541 West Broadway
Forest Lake, MI 55025
e-mail: ncyama@worldnet.att.net
web site: www.ncyama.org
888-NCYAMA-1 phone for membership and marketing
612-464-5494 fax

St. John Eudes Center
Ron Bagley, C.J.M., Director
36 Flohr Ave.
West Seneca, NY 14224
e-mail: eudescenter@compuserve.com
716-825-4319 phone